DON'T THROW

—— THE ——

BOOK AT THEM

DON'T THROW
——— THE ———
BOOK AT THEM

COMMUNICATING THE CHRISTIAN MESSAGE
TO PEOPLE WHO DON'T READ

HARRY BOX

WILLIAM CAREY
LIBRARY

CONTENTS

LIST OF FIGURES

LIST OF ABBREVIATIONS

DMiss
Doctorate of Missiology

GR
Gospel Recordings (Incorporated)

GRN
Global Recordings Network

MA
Master of Arts

PLO
Palestinian Liberation Organisation

PNG
Papua New Guinea

SIM
SIM (International)—formerly Sudan Interior Mission

WBT/SIL
Wycliffe Bible Translators / Summer Institute of Linguistics

FOREWORD

This is a brilliant book. It deals with a long neglected topic that affects Christian missions in most of the world. An estimated two-thirds or more of the world's peoples don't read, many because they have not learned to read, many because they can read but don't choose to. Yet most mission organizations assume that nonliterates need to learn to read if they are serious about their Christian commitment.

To reach nonliterates, missionaries have two possible approaches: either teach them to read, or learn to communicate in ways familiar to the groups to be reached. Mission organizations have tended toward the first of these alternatives, starting schools to teach children and, in the process, bypassing the traditional communicational structures. In our area of northeastern Nigeria, our message was largely understood as an appeal to children and those who chose to westernize. Becoming a Christian was often seen as synonymous with learning to read. As an old man once said to me, "I'd like to become a Christian, but I'm too old to learn to read."

The problem of missionary approaches that are less than maximally effective because too dependent on literacy is what Dr. Box is addressing here. He is concerned that we understand how things look to nonliterate peoples and how to approach them effectively without being tied to literacy. Though his field experience has been among oral learners in Papua New Guinea, his presentation has a much wider base. He has scoured the relevant literature for both case studies and principles of application.

One of the strong points of Box's presentation is his application of cultural and communicational principles to the task of reaching people within their frame of reference. Nonliterates are adults, not children. They are able to think clearly and logically, though their logic is often based on different assumptions than ours. And their approach to life and thinking is more like that of the authors of Scripture than ours is.

It is our task, then, to learn their approach and concerns and adapt our presentations to those rather than to attempt to extract them from their context in order to win them to Christ. We should learn the communicational structures as well as the language and culture of our receptors. If we are to follow Jesus' example, we need to be incarnational rather than extractionist, honouring nonliterates as worthy whether or not they ever learn to read.

This is a critique of standard mission policy and of our ethnocentric approach to communication.

We have much to learn. We need to understand the characteristics of oral communication and to use them, honouring the people by entering into their communicational world. Oral communicators are usually storytellers, often weaving singing and drama into their stories. Every point can be made with a story. We Westerners *illustrate* with stories. They *drive their points home* with stories. And, interestingly enough, when we use stories, even among Westerners, we are more effective than when we simply state our points. Indeed, memory specialists tell us that we (even literates) record the events of our lives in pictures, often embodied in stories. I believe what we learn by studying how oral communicators function helps us understand communication in general, whether literate or nonliterate. Though our focus may be on literacy, it is the nonliterate factors that are basic and enable truly effective communication.

Dr. Box is not against literacy. Indeed, in his later chapters he discusses how best to work toward literacy without making it a requirement for church membership. Before he turns to that subject, though, he deals in a masterful way with understanding oral communicators and the types of communicational techniques they employ. He has also asked and answered the question, why didn't Jesus write a book? He then deals with the fact that the Old Testament, even though written, was largely presented in an oral communication style.

Next Dr. Box presents the theory of communication that lies behind his analysis, followed by a series of cases exemplifying effective use of oral communication techniques in several societies. Box then turns to the very important topic of how to produce Christian leaders without depending on literacy. His next topic is the relationships between literacy and oral communication, followed by a scheme to develop an effective nonliteracy-based approach to an oral society.

As I've stated above, I consider this book to be a brilliant presentation of the case for approaching oral societies without depending on literacy. Box shows high respect for oral communicators and their methods of communication. He is skilful in his application of our best understandings of communication theory to the topic of oral communication.

In my own ministry among an oral people I saw in action some of the principles Dr. Box is presenting. We were pioneer missionaries in northeastern Nigeria. One of our approaches to evangelism was to send out evangelists into the villages in our area to contact village chiefs asking permission to hear the gospel presented. On one occasion an evangelist reported the following.

He and his ministry group were in a village on the top of a nearby mountain that had not heard the gospel before. So, after they had gotten the chief's permission and a small crowd had gathered, they had begun to sing one of the Christian songs created (not written) by the Christians in the Christian community in the valley. Shortly after the evangelist team had started singing, the chief stopped them. The evangelist reporting this said his thought was that they were going to be chased out of that village. However, that's not what happened. After stopping the singing, the chief asked the evangelist, "Where did you learn this song? Our girls have been singing it for months during their dances when the moon is full. Who is this Yesu Kristi that they are singing about?"

The songs honouring Jesus had been the primary evangelist, opening up this mountain village to the gospel. Our strategy had been to encourage the production and use of these memorized indigenous songs rather than to create a songbook that people could read. In this example and in many others, the approach of being positive toward their oral culture and working within it rather than through literacy paid great dividends. Not unrelated to this approach is the fact that that tribal group of 400,000 is about 95 percent Christian now.

It is results like this that Dr. Box wants to see as communicators of the gospel learn to use the communicational structures already in the culture rather than teach oral peoples to depend on foreign approaches such as literacy.

We need to be receptor oriented, feeding Christian messages into their forms of communication, not denying the value of literacy-based communication but not depending so heavily on literacy that we ignore or downplay the use of traditional communicational vehicles.

Westernization has more than doubled the number of cultures in the world. In each society nowadays there are westernizing segments and traditional segments. Western missionary efforts have focused on reaching those who want to westernize. Their culture is valid, and these people should be reached in terms of their westernized culture, which depends heavily on literacy. But what about the billions of traditionalists who will never learn to read? They need to learn about a Jesus who came all the way down into the life and culture of a people much like themselves, honouring their ways of thinking and behaving as adequate vehicles for their response to him.

It is out of respect for the traditional oral communicators of the world and their need to be reached in familiar ways that Harry Box has written this excellent book. May God bless it and use it to enable us who are hampered by our literate ways to escape and gain the freedom to appreciate and use the oral tools so precious to most of the peoples of the world.

Charles H. Kraft
South Pasadena, California

INTRODUCTION

There are many situations around the world today where Western Christians are involved in a cross-cultural presentation of the Christian message. Generally this presentation is based on books and other literacy materials and follows a time-oriented, rationalistic style of reasoning that is typical of Western society. In other words, we "throw the book at them"!

However, the people receiving this presentation are usually oral communicators who are event-oriented and likely to be concrete relational thinkers. As a result, the message is often not clearly understood and the audience response not encouraging. In such situations, the issue we need to consider very carefully is whether a literacy-based presentation is the best or even a good strategy to follow. Should we rather be presenting a message that is based on the thinking patterns and communication forms of the people who are actually receiving that message?

The emphasis placed on the use of literature in evangelism, in both monocultural and cross-cultural situations, implies the belief held in Western societies that there is some sort of inevitability about everyone becoming literate someday. Literature distribution, and especially Scripture distribution, is seen as the most effective way to communicate the Christian message to people.

In seeking to communicate the Christian message we are not dealing with grade one primers, but rather with adult-level material that requires a mature level of both reading and comprehension skills. Standards of literacy vary considerably from country to country, which makes it difficult to work out just what it means to be "literate." This means that many people who may be classified as literate in a particular society would find it extremely difficult to understand the Christian message if it were only presented to them in the form of literature.

Another factor often overlooked is that many people who become literate through an educational program may return to a society where there are practically no books or magazines, and no demand for them to continue with their literacy skills. As a result they revert to being nonliterate. This means that the facts about what is actually happening in the world in relation to literacy are often confused with what people expect to be happening.

It is not the intention of this book to question the value of literacy. There are many good reasons for people becoming literate, and the whole issue of literacy in oral societies is considered carefully in a later chapter (see ch. 8). However, what this book *is* saying is that if we want to communicate the Christian message to people who do not read, then a literacy-based strategy is probably not the best way to go.

The facts are that the great majority of people in the world today are oral communicators. As Alex Smith notes, "Despite many libraries full of books, multitudes of magazines on multiple subjects, myriads of daily newspapers, much cyberspace media through emails, text messaging, worldwide websites, personal blogs, and so forth, the reality is that most of the current world's population of six and a half billion residents, functions primarily in the realm of orality. . . . Avery Willis of the Southern Baptist's International Mission Board declares, 'Seventy percent of the world's people today can't, don't or won't read' (Jewell 2006:56)" (2008, 2–3). This percentage is particularly significant in those areas of the world labelled "developing countries," which are also those places that are the least evangelized with the gospel of Christ. In describing people as oral communicators, I am referring not only to those people who cannot read or write, but also to those who may have some literacy skills but whose primary orientation is to oral communication.

Something else that reinforces the "throw the book at them" strategy has been the great acceleration of industrial, economic, political, and scientific progress during the past four centuries in Western society. This led to the colonization of many countries by Western nations, and the introduction of Western philosophies and education systems into those countries. This coincided with the great expansion of the modern missionary movement, which brought many thousands of missionaries from Western countries to non-Western ones, bearing with them the message of Christianity. As a consequence it has become an accepted strategy for many Christian cross-cultural communicators to use the Western education system of literacy and formal training, along with the provision of the Scriptures in printed form, as the best way to bring the gospel to people who do not read. Closely linked with that, and also probably felt even more strongly, is the concept that this is also the best way to train nonliterate Christians to become Christian leaders.

This type of communication strategy has been modified considerably over recent years as more and more cross-cultural missionaries are taking advantage of training and insights that encourage them to think primarily about their audience when they are making their presentation of the Christian message. That is, they can perceive that with nonliterate people it is important to use oral communication forms and techniques that are part of the people's own culture. In spite of this, there still remains a basic conviction on the part of many cross-cultural missionaries that, although there are other useful options, the Western-oriented literacy/literature-based formal education system is the *best* system to use to bring God's message to people in an oral society, and particularly to train them to become Christian leaders.

Part of the reason for this kind of approach to cross-cultural communication is that many Western, literacy-oriented people consider oral communicators to be inferior to themselves. This concept of superiority relates primarily to intellectual capacity and learning ability, but also shows itself in general paternalism and a tendency to treat adult oral communicators as children in both evangelistic and leadership training programs. The problem is also one of worldview, and highlights the fundamental differences of worldview between oral and literacy-oriented people.

The facts are that oral communicators have just the same intellectual capacity and learning ability as literates. Their learning skills and communication techniques may be quite different, but they are just as capable as literates of receiving and understanding the full range of Christian teaching. However, as oral communicators, the way they process this information in their minds will be different from the way literates do it.

I will seek to demonstrate in this book that where people are members of an oral society, or where this is still the primary orientation of the society, then the oral communication techniques that are part of that people's own culture are the most appropriate ones to use in the communication of Christian truths to these people. These are also the most appropriate for training these people to become Christian leaders in their own society.

In support of this proposal, this book also looks at some of the examples in Scripture of how God communicated his message to people. We see that Jesus' messages in the Gospels, and also the original presentation of the Old Testament Scriptures, were all prepared for oral communicators and presented to those people by means of oral communication forms. These precedents of Scripture provide excellent models for those people who are considering development of a strategy for communicating God's word to oral societies. It is also clearly shown why Jesus didn't write a book or attempt to communicate his teaching by means of literacy and literature. Rather he used the oral communication system that was appropriate for his audience and, in particular, his disciples. The fact that Jesus Christ, the Son of God, used certain communication principles and techniques to present his message of eternal salvation to the people among whom he lived demands our special attention. Those people were oral communicators, and so this makes the whole ministry of Jesus extremely relevant to Christian cross-cultural communication today.

1

UNDERSTANDING ORAL COMMUNICATORS

Making a clear definition of who exactly are the oral communicators of the world is not a straightforward matter. We may sometimes refer to them as illiterates, preliterates, or nonreaders, but these are negative ideas, and unfortunately this is the way Western, literacy-oriented society usually regards them. A more positive way to view them is to say that they are oral people who respond primarily to oral messages and to the people and events within their society.

We can also consider as oral communicators those people who are part of a literate society and are themselves functionally literate, but who for most situations do not choose to use their literacy skills. These people have been described simply as "non-book" people, and will be discussed in more detail in later chapters. Though I will be referring primarily to people who are functionally nonliterate, I feel it is important for us to realize that there is a significant group of people who are part of Western literate society but who can still be regarded as oral communicators.

In general, the statistics relating to literacy are not clearly defined, as the standards used for classifying people as literate vary considerably. Statistics from organisations such as the World Health Organisation and UNESCO tend to be very much on the high side. "Developing" countries in particular are under pressure to demonstrate that literacy is increasing within their borders. However, adult literacy programs within these countries may only require that people attain a level of literacy whereby they can read a few simple words and sentences.

In "developed" countries also, statistics are not always what they seem to be. These countries would not want it widely known if literacy rates were lower than expected or else declining. In the United States and Australia, for example, official figures would indicate that 99 percent of their populations are literate. However, both these countries acknowledge that at least 10 percent of their people are nonliterate, and they have special programs to encourage these people to become literate.

But when we are thinking about communicating the gospel message to people, we also need to realize we are looking for more than just basic literacy skills. Although the Bible does contain some simple material, much of it requires an advanced level of reading. Many people could be regarded as functionally literate and still have great difficulty in reading their Bible with comprehension. For these people, it is the oral presentation of the Christian message that will be relevant and meaningful, and "throwing the book at them" will not have much significance at all.

Putting it all together, if we consider those people who belong to predominantly oral societies as well as the "non-book" people of literate societies, we are probably looking at something like 70 percent of the world's present population. This is an enormous number of people who are best described as oral communicators.[1]

It is also important for us to understand that this group of people includes a high percentage of the non-Christian people of the world and also a high percentage of the unevangelized people of the world. In the light of these facts, if we are at all interested in having an effective ministry of communicating the Christian message to these people, then understanding oral communicators, their characteristics, and their methods of communication demands our serious consideration.

---

1   Klem (1982, 8–25) gives a very comprehensive treatment of the matter of how to assess people as "literate"—and what that means. He also discusses the criteria for "functional literacy" and how this is determined. His conclusion is that the vast majority of the world's people are oral communicators. These comments were made some years ago, but I believe Klem's premises are still very relevant.

SOME THINGS WE SHOULD KNOW ABOUT ORAL COMMUNICATION

The following aspects of oral communication are important for us to understand as a basic approach to this topic.

It is a worldwide system. In many parts of the world today there is a strong oral system of communication. For the majority of the world's people this is the traditional system of communication that people have used for many hundreds of years. This oral system is not just something superficial, only for passing simple messages; rather it is a complex system requiring many skills. This system is able to communicate at all levels of the society and to all situations. It is at the heart of all experiences (see Klem 1982, xix).

It is a traditional method of celebration. In this case drama and dance are often used alongside singing and chanting, along with drums, didgeridoo, rhythm sticks, and many other forms of musical accompaniment. Oral communities usually have many reasons for celebration, and so this type of communication forms an important part of their life experience (see ibid., 126–38; Finnegan 1970; Nicholls 1983, 1–12).

It is a traditional method of teaching. For many societies, oral communication is used to give all instruction about religious beliefs, kinship systems, social structure, and the obligations required by the community. Cultural values and moral code, and practical things like hunting, fishing, and house building, are also taught this way. This oral instruction is usually accompanied by personal example and modelling. Klem gives many examples of this (see 1982, 97–109).

There is a wide diversity of oral communication. There are many different ways of using the oral communication system. These include many types of storytelling, drama, poetry, singing, and music. Some of these oral media are unique to a particular group; others are shared by many groups. Oral people are not limited in their oral skills or in the sort of communication that they can produce.

As we examine the evidence of the oral media that are used today, we find that there is incredible variety and creativity. The following are some writers who give an extensive range of examples of oral communication techniques:

- Denoon and Lacey 1981: Poetic mnemonic devices, navigation, stories, paintings, buildings, tombs, dance, music, and ritual
- Farrall 1984: Navigation in Micronesia

- Finnegan 1970: Poems, stories, songs, connected with divination boards. Praise songs, proverbs, riddles
- Horton 1967: Epic songs, love poetry, magical rites
- Klem 1982: Songs, hymns, stories, riddles, jokes, chants, dances, proverbs, poems
- Nicholls 1983: Poetry, storytelling, proverbs, songs, drama, dance, puppetry
- Pearson 1977: Storytelling with sandgraphs

Oral communication requires live performers and audience response. The oral system of communication is different from the written system in that the oral system requires a live performer or performers who can use all kinds of facial expressions, gestures, and sounds, and may also have musical background. In many cases the person who is skilled in oral communication has an important position in society.

Oral communication also requires an audience and, in most cases, active participation by the audience. The performer of a story or poem or song looks to the audience for an appropriate response—to participate in a chorus line, or in some other way to become involved in the whole presentation (see Dorson 1972, 41; Klem 1982, 107–8).

What we have considered above is really just a brief look at some of the aspects of oral communication. These form an introduction to the more detailed study below of the prominent characteristics of oral communicators. The purpose of this is that we might grasp the significance of these facts: that oral communication is widespread, involving billions of people; that it totally permeates the lifestyle and communication experience of those people; and that in many cases it is very different from everything related to literacy-oriented experience.

CHARACTERISTIC FEATURES OF ORAL COMMUNICATORS

In considering the characteristic features of oral communicators, we are not simply considering the features of a particular culture, but rather some particular features that are common to many cultures. These features relate directly to communication and are particularly significant in the area of cross-cultural communication.

Group Orientation

This is perhaps the most obvious of all the characteristics of oral communicators, as the very nature of oral communication demands the presence of more than one person to participate, and in many cases a group of people. But the fact that it is obvious does not mean that people always understand the significance of this characteristic. Group orientation is the basis for all the other characteristics that we will consider, and to understand this characteristic fully means that we have a good grasp on understanding oral communicators as a whole and how we can communicate effectively with them. As Ong writes, "Oral communication unites people in groups. Writing and reading are solitary activities" (1982, 69). This is easily observed in contact with either a literacy-oriented or oral communication group.

Group orientation affects every part of oral people's lives. It determines cultural values as well as the social, political, educational, spiritual, and economic activities of each person in the community. In all of these things the group is in focus, not the individual. Also, and very significantly in respect to Christian communication, it affects decision-making processes. Group decisions are usually regarded as more important and more binding on the individual than personal decisions (see ch. 9). As we examine further the characteristics of oral people, we will see just how thoroughly this primary characteristic of group orientation permeates each one.

An important feature of this characteristic is the very strong, and in many cases complete, contrast to the individualism that is characteristic of literacy-oriented people. This contrast is often recognized by literacy-oriented people, but in most cases the serious significance of it is not realized. This is especially important with regard to communication of the Christian message. For Christian communicators who are literacy-oriented people, a proper understanding of this group orientation characteristic is essential if they hope to achieve effective communication to oral people. The following characteristics are closely related to this one and merit our close attention.

Event-oriented Rather than Time-oriented

Probably one of the first things that is noticed by someone from a Western, time-oriented culture when visiting an oral, event-oriented culture is the marked difference in the perspective on time. In some cases it may help the

Westerner to relax and enjoy personal relationships more fully, but in most cases it results in irritation on the Westerner's part as he or she worries about people not doing things "on time" and not making "full use" of their time.

For the Westerner, time is a linear concept, marked off in precise increments and stretching from a historic but rather insignificant past into a rapidly advancing and highly focused future. For the oral person, however, time is the ever-present *now*, and is measured not in linear terms but in terms of one's involvement in the events that are happening in his or her own community. Also, he is not so concerned about whether those events begin and end at certain times, but rather that they are completed satisfactorily. Very often this time focus is on the past and the people and events that are memorable, but only as these have relevance for the present. Sometimes he looks to the future, but again, only as it has relevance to the present, and this is usually in terms of preparations that need to be made for anticipated events, such as weddings and festivals.

So we can understand that an oral person's perception of time, one of the fundamental aspects of any person's worldview, is clearly and markedly different from that of a literacy-oriented person. It is vitally important to bear this in mind, not only in our personal approach and relationships with oral people but especially in the preparation and presentation of any Christian messages.

The Contrast between Aural and Visual Orientation

For people whose only experience has been that of a literate society, it is very difficult to understand why people in an oral culture don't instantly recognize pictures or drawings on a page. Westerners think, well of course people can "see" that! We also tend to persevere with visual and print-oriented communication to oral people because of a basic assumption that it is not really going to be a big problem for people to adjust from the aural to the visual.

In an oral culture, words are not visual items, even though they may be describing something visual. Words are aural happenings or events. Once they are expressed they are gone. They can be memorized and recalled, but they cannot be displayed, stored, and retrieved in the visual way that occurs in a literate society. Such a concept is quite foreign to oral societies.

Ong points out that in Western society, for many centuries now, our philosophical and scientific understanding of the physical universe has been described in purely visual terms. But studies of oral cultures have shown that there are other options open to us: "There are cultures that encourage their members to think of the universe less than we do as something picturable and more than we do as a harmony, something held together as a sound or group of sounds, a symphony, is held together" (1969, 636). The people of these cultures seek to live in harmony with their universe rather than attempting to analyse and control it.

The world of an oral culture is an event world rather than an object world. It is a world of traditionalism, where the preservation of tradition is the key to the preservation of cultural identity and history. It is a world of debate, discussion, and consensus, where learning takes place in the context of highly developed forms of oral expression and memory retention. Advances in understanding and cultural development do not come as the result of discoveries put forward by individuals who have prepared their ideas in private, like Einstein or Aristotle; rather progress is made more slowly as everyone advances together.

These features of an oral society help us to understand a little more clearly why ancestors and past events are so important in these societies; why song, music, and dance are such priorities; why meetings in the "men's house" extend for such lengthy periods; and why people are so hesitant to step out and be different from the group. Such behaviours are not just hobbies or means of entertainment, nor are they particular personality quirks due to a lack of "education." No—rather they are important features demonstrating that there are viable alternatives to the Western cultural perception of reality. This is a challenge to Westerners not only to reconsider the way we perceive our own society, but also in the way we evaluate the perceptions, forms, and processes of other cultures.

This focus of oral cultures on sound has important consequences as we consider the next characteristic of their worldview.

The Acquisition and Preservation of Knowledge by Oral Rather than Literate Means

Oral cultures are often perceived in a negative way by people from literate cultures; that is, they are considered nonliterate, non-book, and uneducated (referring to formal, Western-type education) societies. This evaluation is based on what these cultures do not have in the way of specific types of knowledge rather than what they do have. However, research continues to reveal the amazing scope and variety of knowledge contained in oral societies.

What we want to establish here is that the acquisition and preservation of knowledge is a primary value in oral cultures, and the manner in which it is done is in marked contrast to the methods of literate societies. As we have already indicated, in many cultures, oral communication is used to give all social, religious, educational, and economic instructions.

People in oral cultures do not "study" in the same way as people in literate cultures. Learning often takes place through apprenticeship: by hunting with experienced hunters, by fishing with experienced fishermen, etc. People learn by listening and repeating what they have heard—for example, proverbs—and then practising different ways of combining and recombining the parts. This is also done with songs, poems, stories, and chants.

There are many techniques for remembering and repeating ancient traditions as well as current gossip. Often this involves intense artistic effort. But these art forms are not used merely for entertainment or artistic expression, as people in Western cultures might use them. Rather there is an oral system that preserves traditions, rewards group loyalty, expresses communal pride, spreads news, gains social approval, and also enjoys a good time with friends. In many cases these oral art forms are accompanied by drama, dance, mime, or puppets.

In oral societies there are many instances where oral poetry takes the place of newspapers. Songs and stories can be used to report and comment on current affairs, to bring about political pressure, for propaganda, and to reflect and mould public opinion (see Ong 1982, 9; Klem 1982, 111; Lindfors and Owomoyela 1973, v; Finnegan 1970, 272).

Among the Hmong people of Laos, the same characteristics are seen in the acquisition of knowledge. Learning takes place in groups, since individuals do not have written materials to study. The Hmong people traditionally learned through doing; even many literate Hmong find that the printed word is not an adequate means of communication, and only a poor substitute for the oral, experiential learning that is done in the traditional society.

Not only is the acquisition of knowledge important in oral communities, but so is the preservation of that knowledge. The social, moral, religious, and in many cases political history of a people is a vital concern and a key factor in maintaining identity as a people. Again, the particular characteristics of oral cultures are demonstrated in the achievement of preserving such a history.

This is where we encounter the feats of memory which are expected in oral societies but which seem to be so amazing to people of literate cultures. People with excellent memories are highly respected and are the most credible members of oral communities. These people are able to recall the highly detailed rituals of their society's traditional ceremonies, or the traditional songs, stories, and poems, which may be numbered in the thousands, or the names associated with debate about their genealogies, which, in Papua New Guinea, can mean tens of thousands of names.

If these memories falter, or are lost, then the people's history and national identity may also be lost. So for it is considered well worthwhile to put considerable time and effort into the acquisition and preservation of material that is important to them. That is why we see strong group support for the constant repetition of these oral items and encouragement of their memorization (see Shuter in Samovar and Porter 1985, 102–8; Klem 1982, 120; Bateson 1958, 222–23).

The Attribution of Power to the Spoken Word

We are not just thinking here of the persuasive force of great speaking and storytelling, although that aspect is certainly part of the way words are used in oral cultures. We are thinking rather of the completely different way that oral people think about words. What we have said above about the significance of sound relates to this issue, but it is more than that too. *Spoken words come from a living source.* In an oral community they are identified with that source and the whole context of that person's existence and relationships. Depending on who the source is, and their significance in that community, the community is acutely aware of the potential for power that resides in those words.

In oral societies language is a mode of action rather than simply a process for identifying people's thoughts. Words are events rather than items. All sounds, and especially spoken words, which come from within a living person are considered to be "dynamic." It is almost universal that oral cultures consider words to have the potential of magical powers. This is in striking contrast to the way words are considered in a literacy-oriented society. People in a literary society would hardly think of words on a page as being "dead," but when we think of the way an oral person would regard those words, that is what they have become.

Klem (1982) and Horton (1967) give us many insights from Africa that point out the significant differences between traditional African thinking and the way Westerners think today. Central to these differences is the concept of words. In Western thought words are merely symbols for sounds, with no power in themselves, but according to Horton, "There is a very general African assumption about the power of words, uttered under appropriate circumstances, to bring into being the events or states they stand for" (ibid., 157). This concept of power in words means that people are very careful and cautious in their use of words in certain situations. They are reluctant to reveal their real names to people they do not know or trust, and they use euphemisms for things such as death and dangerous diseases. Much of this is also related to the people's understanding of the spirit forces at work behind nature, responding to the utterances of words, even if they are spoken by accident or carelessly.

Another evidence of this in Africa is seen in the keen interest people display in blessings. Even Muslim leaders opposed to Christianity will be quite happy for an African Christian or an expatriate missionary to pray a blessing on their homes. But to speak in conversation about the possibility of a person's death, and their consequent need of eternal salvation, would possibly threaten the safety of the speaker. Because of their view of the power of words about events to cause them to happen, oral people have a strong dislike of even mentioning evil events that could possibly happen.

If we can understand this concept that oral people have about words and their power, it helps us to appreciate the high value they place on the use of words in all of the occasions that make up the context of their lives: births, marriages, and deaths; preparing for battle with an enemy; hunting, fishing, and farming; sickness and misfortune; fear of evil spirits; and many more. The spoken word has the potential to meet all their needs.

When we turn to the Christian Scriptures, we find many accounts that indicate that this same characteristic was evident among the Israelite people. This was not so much a concept of power in the spoken word of the people themselves, but more so in the power of their God to bring about everything he said he would do. This is seen especially in the creation of the universe as being an event in which God spoke and it was done. "And God said . . ." is the key phrase in Genesis 1 that describes this activity. This is also summarised in Psalm 33:

By the word of the LORD the heavens were made,
their starry host by the breath of his mouth.
For he spoke, and it came to be;
he commanded, and it stood firm. (vv. 6,9)

Throughout the Old Testament the phrase "according to the word of the Lord" signals the activity of God. God declares his intention through an oral statement, and the testimony of the Scriptures is that he always does what he says. The climax of God's message to people is declared in Hebrews 1:1–3, where it says that God has spoken to us by his Son. John 1:1 tells us that Jesus, God's Son, is the *Logos*, the Word. This is not simply referring to an oral message, although it does include that. The concept of the "Word" implies a living word. Everything that Jesus was, everything he said, and everything he did, was God's message to the world.

This concept of a living word gives us a real clue as to the understanding oral people have about the spoken word. For them the spoken word is always a living word, identified with a living person, and as such carries great potential to bring about what has been spoken. This is in marked contrast to the general perception of the spoken and written word by literacy-oriented people. For them the value or power of the spoken or written word is found in its own content and structure and may not even be associated with its author. In many cases the spoken or written word is regarded as being completely neutral, not having any power or influence, simply being a channel of information.

It is important for Western Christian communicators to understand this basic perception of the spoken word by oral people and the great contrast to its perception by literacy-oriented people. This should have a major influence on how we plan and carry out our communication strategy.

FURTHER CHARACTERISTICS OF ORAL THOUGHT AND EXPRESSION

The following characteristics have been gleaned from Walter J. Ong's book *Orality and Literacy* (1982). Each of these insights helps us to build up a more complete understanding of the oral person's worldview. The following are based on an awareness of the fact that the thought and expression in primary oral cultures are expected to be recalled by the memory.

"Add-on," "Build-up" Structures Rather than "Cause-and-Effect"

The information is given layer upon layer rather than with logical sequences: "And . . . and . . . and . . ." instead of "therefore." Grammar is not developed in the concise, sequential manner familiar to those in literate cultures.

A familiar example of this "add-on" style of oral expression is in the creation narrative of Genesis 1:1–31. In the Authorised (King James) Version there is a total of ninety-five uses of the word "and." Seventy-two of those are used in an introductory capacity. To contemporary, literacy-oriented people this narrative sounds cumbersome and archaic, but for oral people it is quite normal and natural.

Jesus also used this characteristic in his teaching. A prominent example of this is his teaching about the kingdom of God. In the Gospels there is no single statement or passage that gives the total teaching about the kingdom of God; rather there are many statements, stories, and illustrations, presented in the "layer upon layer" style, and it is only as these are all added together that people can see the complete picture.

> The kingdom of heaven is like a man who sowed good seed in his field. . . .
> The kingdom of heaven is like a mustard seed. . . .
> The kingdom of heaven is like yeast. . . .
> The kingdom of heaven is like treasure hidden in a field. . . .
> The kingdom of heaven is like a net. . . . (Matt 13:24,31,33,44,47)

This is not the way literacy-oriented people would have done it, but it is perfectly normal and very understandable to an oral community.

Collective Description Rather than Precise Analysis

Oral people prefer the sound of a cluster of words to describe certain things rather than one precisely chosen term. This concept is closely tied to oral people's reliance on formulas and familiar clusters of words and expressions to help their memorization of these materials. For instance, in their traditional stories, they would not talk about the soldier, but the *brave* soldier; not simply the princess, but the *beautiful, young* princess. This is part of the reason why much of oral literature is so lengthy, and is often rejected by literates as cumbersome and tedious.

Familiar clichés such as "enemies of the people" and "capitalist warmongers," which have been used in political addresses to people in developing countries, may seem absurd to literacy-oriented people, but they actually strike a very resonant chord with the thought processes of oral people, who are quickly able to store these in their memories.

Traditional expressions and formulas are carefully guarded, not consciously, but by constant repetition and a strong reluctance to change an expression once it has become established. It is hard work getting these expressions and formulas together over the generations, and therefore they are not lightly discarded. Oral people generally have nowhere to store them outside their minds, so breaking up these expressions by analysis is a high-risk procedure that may cause them to be lost altogether.

The characteristic of collective description is probably not quite as common in the Scriptures as in fictional types of oral literature. Nevertheless, there are still many examples—for instance, in the Old Testament, "stiffnecked people" (Ex 32:9 AKJV) and "uncircumcised Philistine" (1 Sam 17:26 AKJV/NIV). In the Gospels, the parable of the talents in Matthew 25:14–46 is very typical oral literature: "good and faithful servant" (v. 21 AKJV/NIV), "wicked and slothful servant" (v. 26 AKJV), and "outer darkness" (v. 30 AKJV).

It is interesting to note that these oral features are preserved more in the literal translation of the Authorised Version than in modern versions that present the Scriptures in contemporary, literacy-oriented English. This characteristic is looked for and appreciated by oral people, but it is usually regarded as tedious by literacy-oriented people, who tend to edit out these features. For Christian communicators working in an oral community, discovering this sort of characteristic requires thorough research, which then has to be followed up by careful preparation of any material presented to that community so that such an oral characteristic is preserved and effectively utilized.

Repetitious

The continuity of oral discourse is aided by frequent reference to what has already been mentioned. This is a feature not only in oral societies but also in literate ones. Any worthwhile speaker will make sure that he or she repeats the main points of his or her address several times in order to ensure that the audience will retain that information. Once that message is put into print, it is trimmed of all such repetitions as being redundant and unnecessary. For the oral community, however, where the printed version will not be available, the repetitions are essential for a satisfactory understanding and acceptance of the message, and for its preservation in the memory. Repetition is not considered "boring" for oral people; repetition of the familiar and well known is highly treasured.

There are numerous reasons for repetition. Sometimes it is for emphasis and sometimes to prompt a response from a group of listeners. Sometimes it is necessary to fit in with the poetic or musical structure of the message. This oral feature is very evident in the Old Testament, particularly in the Writings: in Psalm 136 the statement "His love endures forever" is repeated twenty-six times, probably as a response by a Levitical choir. It is also noticeable in the Gospels: in Matthew 23:13–32, the statement "Woe to you, teachers of the law and Pharisees, you hypocrites!" is repeated six times.

Literacy-oriented people feel quite uncomfortable with all these repetitions and would prefer to remove them. The converse is also true, that in presenting material to be taught, literacy-oriented people would not think of adding this feature. Yet for oral people this characteristic is normal, expected, and an important part of learning and remembering.

How often do Western Christian communicators feel the strong urge to edit out "unnecessary" words and phrases from a message in order that it should not become tedious or boring? The three characteristics above indicate that it could be those very words and phrases that make the message relevant and dynamic to an oral audience. Only careful research and understanding of the oral communication system will enable the communicator to come up with the right formulation.

Conservative or Traditionalist

Knowledge preserved in an oral culture has been gained at great cost, through much repetition and mental effort, both by individuals and the community. Such knowledge is not going to be lightly tossed aside for something new or different that comes along. That which is well known and approved is highly valued. In such oral communities the elders play an important information role which is not necessary in a literate society.

Jesus demonstrated his knowledge of this characteristic when he linked his new teachings with the old traditional ones as an effective teaching technique. In Matthew 5:27 Jesus says, "You have heard that it was said, 'You shall not commit adultery.' But I tell you that anyone who looks at a woman lustfully has already committed adultery with her in his heart." The traditional teaching was known and respected. The new teaching was placed alongside it, not to replace it, but to be a progression and fulfilment. In this way the traditional teaching acted as a memory aid, and the new teaching was accepted because of its link with the old.

Closely Related to People's Everyday Living

Oral cultures must think of and express all their knowledge in reference to their immediate context. Everything must be explainable and believable in terms of present-day activities, events, and language. Abstract terms and ideas are not a prominent part of oral cultures. Trades and skills are not learned from manuals, but through apprenticeship to skilled older people. Jesus demonstrated this feature very clearly in his use of parables and stories that dealt with the objects of his audience's everyday world, such as sheep and shepherds (John 10:1–18), oil and lamps (Matt 25:1–13), sparrows (Matt 10:29–31), and mustard seed (Matt 13:31,32). He taught his disciples by the apprenticeship method, out in the villages, by the seashore, and in the fields.

This characteristic of oral people is relatively easy for literate observers to see and understand. But it is much more difficult for those same people to use that characteristic as they communicate to oral people, rather than the abstract, text-based forms with which they are familiar. But if the ministry of communicating the Christian message to oral people is going to be effective, then it is a characteristic that needs to become an essential part of that message.

Graphic Description of Conflict, Struggle, and Praise

One of the skills that is appreciated in a literate culture is that of the actor or poet who presents his performance with full expression of the emotion and conflict that truly characterize the particular story or ballad. If he is able to hold the attention of the audience and make them "feel" the drama of the situation and identify with the struggles of the characters, then he is regarded as being very successful. This is what we call *agonistic* expression. But if anyone in a literate culture were to express themselves in the same dramatic, confrontational way in their everyday situation, they would be regarded as abnormal.

In an oral society, however, this is part of everyday experience, as all types of oral expression, and particularly oral performance, reveal clearly the emotions and struggles of daily life. Physical violence is often described with great enthusiasm, as is also the praise and honour given to heroes and deities. This sort of characteristic is seen in much of the Old Testament, especially the Psalms, where "fulsome praise" is given to God, and where the deep inner feelings of people are graphically expressed (as in Psalm 51). It is also evident in the Gospels, where, in a passage such as the parable of the tenants (Luke 20:9–19), Jesus speaks vividly about God's desire to care for Israel and their stubborn rejection of him, culminating in Jesus' own violent death. The Jewish leaders recognized that Jesus spoke this story against them and, as a result, tried to arrest him.

Literacy-oriented people would tend to feel that these presentations are too emotional and too direct and would prefer something more restrained. But for the oral person such a presentation would lose its dynamic.

Empathy and Participation Rather than Remote Observation

The person in an oral culture is absorbed in the activities and events going on around her or him. Withdrawal from everyday situations and simply observing things as a spectator are not features of oral society. By contrast, in a literate society, writing can separate the writer from what is known and experienced, so that that person can see matters "objectively"; that is, without personal participation.

A key feature of Jesus' training program with his disciples was that it was in total harmony with the oral culture in which he lived. His training was carried out in the midst of people's everyday activities and experiences, not in some remote place of seclusion. Jesus identified himself with the people in their everyday needs and concerns and taught his disciples to do this also.

Economy of Preservation of Oral Culture/History/ Literature

Although oral societies are vitally interested in the people and events of the past, they are also under great pressure from the present to preserve only what is absolutely relevant. Because of the complex skills and mental effort required to preserve oral information, anything that is not regarded as essential by the present community will soon disappear.

There are no libraries or dictionaries in oral cultures; everything must be carried in the mind. Songs, stories, genealogies, and ceremonies may be long and complex, but there is certainly no "padding." Anything that is regarded as not being absolutely necessary for the value of a particular piece of oral expression, or for its process of memorization, will soon be discarded.

This is one of the reasons why the oral teaching of Jesus was so remarkable. Knowing full well this characteristic of the oral Jewish culture, he was prepared to risk his message of eternal life and salvation to the possibility of significant loss or erosion through the normal information-preserving processes of that culture. He did not provide a written backup text, but trusted that his message would be perceived by people as sufficiently relevant and important that they would make the necessary effort to preserve it in their oral tradition.

This is a commendable goal for all Christian communicators to oral people, that the message they present will be perceived by their audience as relevant and important enough that they will want to make the effort to preserve it and pass it on by oral, traditional means.

Focus Is on Event/Situation/Action Rather than Abstract Concepts

People in oral cultures generally do not separate or distance themselves from the situation in which they are involved or which they are discussing. They discuss things in terms of actions and events to which they can relate rather than adopt abstract concepts or attempt to make a series of logical deductions. They also find it difficult to respond to questions from literacy-oriented people, which are typically of an analytical and deductive nature, as they try to "totalize" the context of the question rather than reply to one dissected portion. Guessing and supposing things that they have never experienced are foreign to their thinking processes. The following is an example: "In the far north, where there is snow, all bears are white. Place X is in the far north, and there is always snow there. What colour are the bears at Place X?" Typical response: "I don't know, I've never been there." In other words, the colour of the bears is determined by being there and seeing them, not by reasoning from an abstract written report.

Many of us prepare messages, have discussions, and seek to communicate the Christian message in a variety of ways to oral people. But if we base our messages on reasoning that has been shaped by literacy rather than the oral characteristics mentioned above, then this should give us much food for thought. There is a strong possibility that we are badly miscommunicating. Our message content and presentation must be based firmly on the characteristics and thought processes of our audience of oral communicators.

PERFORMANCE AND PARTICIPATION

The characteristics of performance and participation have been mentioned above, but it is good at this point to emphasise that these are what is so distinctive about oral cultures and the way they view the world.

When an oral communicator thinks about receiving a message, he thinks about a person or group presenting that message orally, in their own cultural way. He doesn't only think about receiving the message but about responding to it, personally and as a member of the community. For him, communication is not only a one-way process. It is an activity in which the whole community can participate.

The whole context of oral communication is radically different from that experienced by people in a literate society. This does not mean that it is any less effective in communicating spiritual truths, but it does mean that Christian cross-cultural communicators who come from a literate society will need to be prepared to make major adjustments to their presentation of the Christian message if they want it to be relevant, acceptable, and dynamic for their oral audience.

CONCLUSION

The information above enables us to establish the following important points concerning oral communicators:

1. *Most of the people in the world are oral communicators.* It is difficult to know exactly how many people are literate and how many are not. There are many different definitions of literacy and functional literacy, and also numerous testing procedures that are used to say just how literate people are. Many people have been through some kind of literacy program, but even so, they still remain oral communicators. We can be reasonably confident

that the majority of people in the world today have the characteristics of oral communicators as described above.

2. *The characteristics of oral communicators are quite distinctive.* These characteristics are not simply related to the people's own culture but relate primarily to the people's basic orientation to oral communication. Each culture expresses these oral characteristics in its own unique way.

3. *There is a marked contrast between the characteristics of oral communicators and those of literacy-oriented people.* This is not simply at a surface level, but rather at a deep worldview level, and is particularly significant in the whole area of communication. To move from an oral worldview position to a literacy-oriented worldview position, or vice versa, requires a major worldview shift.

What this means for the Western Christian cross-cultural communicator is that there are many possibilities for misunderstanding and miscommunication between oral and literacy-oriented people. This is a problem that can be overcome, as we will see. However, we must recognize that there is a definite contrast between the way oral and literate people communicate and that there is a strong possibility of real difficulties arising as literacy-oriented people try to present a message to oral communicators. This must be allowed for in any plan people may have to communicate the Christian message to oral people.

For any communication plan to be effective among oral people, it will need to consider first the characteristics of oral people as described above and the communication forms that they use in their own culture. Understanding how oral people think and communicate is a complex process that will require careful study over a long period of time. This becomes more evident to us in the next chapter as we consider in greater detail the incredible diversity of communication skills in oral communities. However, the important points listed above are able to form a sound basis for our plan to communicate the Christian message to oral people. As this research is applied in Christian outreach to oral people, the results are strikingly effective and most rewarding.

2

CONTEMPORARY ORAL COMMUNITIES AND THEIR COMMUNICATIONAL SKILLS

Having considered the point that there is a significant majority of the world's population who are oral communicators, another very relevant question is often raised by Western Christian communicators: do oral societies have a system of communication that is adequate for receiving and passing on the Christian message?

ORAL COMMUNICATION SKILLS

In this chapter we will describe just briefly some of the communicational skills that are present in oral societies. In so doing we will attempt to provide a glimpse of the rich and varied array of communication that is normally a part of an oral community.

Storytelling[2]

Storytelling is common to all cultures, but the way stories are told, and the reasons for telling them, vary considerably between cultures. This is

---

2   A comprehensive treatment of biblical storytelling in oral cultures, with some excellent case studies, is found in Koehler (2010).

particularly noticeable between literate and oral cultures. In literate cultures storytelling is regarded more as entertainment and seen mostly as a way of telling stories to young children, whereas in oral cultures, while it is still entertaining, storytelling is very much an adult occupation, and is one of the means of preserving the cultural heritage of the people. The following are just a few examples:

The Indian Storyteller

Kath Nicholls describes just how popular this form of communication is in India, where a crowd will quickly gather in a village whenever someone starts to tell a story. The stories usually relate to life in the villages and may give explanations of different facets of nature, such as what causes an earthquake, or be used to teach cultural values and behaviour. Animals often appear in the stories, with human characteristics of stupidity, cunning, gentleness, and courage. In most cases Indian storytelling is accompanied by music.

One of the storytelling styles that is widely accepted and used is Katha-Kalakshepam. In this communicative medium a story or religious discourse is told, sung and intoned by a singer who keeps the rhythm for himself with castinets. The singer requires stamina as he must speak and sing for several hours. He should also act out his story.

In rural Rajasthan, Gujarat and Haryana, the bhopa and his wife are traditional singers of heroic themes. He stretches a long scroll or pad between two poles and on this pad the audience can look at paintings of episodes from the life of the hero as the story is sung. The wife lights up each scene with a lantern as he sings. . . .

The story box or kavad is another visual aid which is popular in Rajasthan and Madhya Pradesh. A number of folding doors open out to reveal the people or episodes of the story as the bhopa sings. This medium is being used today to teach such things as family planning, nutrition and rat control. (Nicholls 1983, 46)

These storytelling techniques are a challenge to Christian communicators to be able to produce Christian messages in story formats that will be just as popular and dynamic as the folk stories are.

Oral Art among the Yoruba People of Nigeria

In West Africa, storytelling is a key part of the practice of divination among the Yoruba people of Nigeria. This is yet another example of the enormous capacity oral communicators have to memorize specific information.

> Another major religious institution revolves around the Ifa priest of divination. He is called Babalawo or father of mysteries. He is supposed to be able to help people and promote healing and is, therefore, sometimes unfortunately called "witchdoctor" by outsiders. Divination is done from a board with sixteen squares or "houses" which are further subdivided to yield a total of sixteen times sixteen or 256. To each of these squares is assigned a number of poems or songs which the diviner must be able to chant accurately. Then for each of these 256 poems or songs there are a large number of stories (ese) called "paths," "roads" or "feet."

> To go into practice a beginner should have learned four stories or myths per odu (song) which would mean a minimum of 1,000 stories. An ideal number of stories for each would be sixteen which would mean a total of 4,096 tales to recite. (Finnegan 1970, 194)

> These songs and stories are not performed openly in public performance, but can be heard by clients who pay for the diviner's services. They are symbolic story texts from which the diviner will deduce the correct sacrifice or course of action for his client to take. The effectiveness and spiritual power of the diviner is thought to be related to his knowledge of the memorized material. (Klem 1982, 133–34)

It is difficult for a literacy-oriented person to appreciate from the bare statistics of this example the considerable amount of time, mental effort, and memorization skill that must be employed by one of these diviners in order to become accomplished in this activity. It is also difficult for a literacy-oriented person to understand the impact on an oral communicator's life when oral skills such as those described above are completely discounted or ignored and literacy-oriented skills are presented as the only ones suitable for learning about Christianity.

Papua New Guinea Storytelling

In Papua New Guinea (PNG) storytelling is also a fine art, with styles varying among the different tribal groups. One publication has a collection of some 140 stories from nineteen different language groups, which is just a minute fraction of what is available among the eight hundred tribal groups in that country. The following is just a small sample of the topics of these stories:

> The Origin of Thunder and Lightning
> Why There Are Mosquitoes
> The Spirit Who Was Hunting for a Wife
> The Woman Who Married a Flying Fox
> The Lizard Who Wanted a Coconut
> How the Birds of Paradise Got Their Tails
> (McElhanon 1982, 9–14)

These stories are the history, traditions, culture, values, religion, philosophy, humour, and tragedy of these people, and much more as well.

I heard about a missionary Bible translator in Papua New Guinea who was working with his language helper on the passage in John 19 about the crucifixion of Jesus. His practice was to record newly translated portions onto cassette and send them around the language group for appraisal. As they started recording, the language helper asked if he could tell the story as they would in his culture. The missionary agreed, and as the language helper told the story of Jesus' crucifixion he interspersed it with loud wailing, very typical of PNG cultural response to death. Having finished the recording, the missionary sent the tapes out to various places. One cassette came to a health clinic where a missionary nurse was attending to a group of women. She set the cassette player up and put the tape in for the women to listen to. When it came to the part with the wailing, she thought it was a bit strange and she turned and smiled. But the women rebuked her and said, "You must not laugh! This is a story about a great man who died!"

This is not an easy technique for a foreigner to learn, but certainly one to be aware of!

Graphic and Plastic Arts

This refers to drawings, paintings, carvings, and sculptures. The variety of this type of communication skill is considerable. The following are two samples of rather distinctive graphic artwork.

Iconographs

The Warlpiri people are a group of nomadic Aborigines located in the central-northern desert area of Australia. They number only a few thousand people, but their tribal territory covers a vast area of many thousands of square miles. They have a rich heritage of cultural arts that are associated with their religious and social life.

Drama, in the form of corroborees, or *purlapas*, is used to relate the stories from the "dream time," the time of their earliest ancestors, and in so doing, to teach their religious laws and social values. Iconographs are also used to relate many of the same stories. These are symbols that can be painted on bark, or on a war shield, or drawn in the sand. Figure 1 shows some examples.

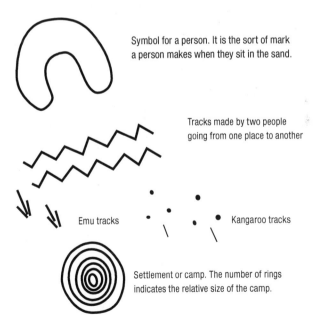

Symbol for a person. It is the sort of mark a person makes when they sit in the sand.

Tracks made by two people going from one place to another

Emu tracks

Kangaroo tracks

Settlement or camp. The number of rings indicates the relative size of the camp.

Fig. 1. Aboriginal iconographs

Even after the coming of the European settlers and missionaries, these sacred stories were kept very much to the Aboriginal people. It was only on rare occasions that a white man would be permitted to view a performance of these sacred corroborees. For many of them, even the Aboriginal women were prohibited from seeing them (see Jordan 1984).

Sandgraphs

Among the VaNgangela people of Angola there is a similar communication form called sandgraphs. The sandgraphs are made on any suitable clear space on the ground. Loose sand and soil are scraped away so that a firm, smooth surface remains. The artist/storyteller then begins by making dots with his fingertips, in precise patterns. When the dot patterns are completed, then the line drawing is done, with a sure hand and definite strokes until the figure is completed. The completed figure is called a *kasona*. Some of the figures are very intricate, and when this is so, the drawing is done in silence, and the story told afterwards. If it is a relatively simple figure, then the story is told as the drawing progresses.

The sandgraphs speak about every aspect of the people's social, family, and religious life, and the religious drawings in particular are most fascinating, in that they are a lasting testimony to the primary religious beliefs of the African people (Pearson 1977, 16). One example is a figure used to represent God.

Fig. 2. Angolan sandgraph: Njambi kalanga—"God"

This figure represents God, "pregnant with creation," existing in eternity before any creation was brought into being. It should be noted that there are two figures intertwined into one in the form of a chrysalis. The informants who supplied this material had no explanation for this.

The top and rear curves, with enclosed dot, represent the heavens, while the lower and frontal curves with their dot depict the earth. The lowest and rear parts with accompanying dot stand for "the pit." They had no explanation of what was meant by "the pit."

The dots that are enclosed singly stand for God's attributes:

"A hasa viose"—He can do all—Omnipotence.
"A tantekeya viose"—He knows all—Omniscience.
"A mona viose"—He sees all—Omnipresence.
"A li na ngozi"—He has goodness—Love.

When asked what the three remaining dots in the middle of the figure meant, the informant said, "We only know that they mean "VuNjambi" (the Godhead). We weren't told anything else." Which is very interesting—a Trinity in the Godhead! (Pearson 1977, 21)

Emil Pearson, who supplied the above information in his book *People of the Aurora*, discovered these sandgraphs when he first came to work as a missionary among the VaNgangela people. He realised the importance of these stories, and the tremendous potential of using them as an introduction to the Christian gospel. He set himself to learn the sandgraph stories, of which there are hundreds, and in time became one of the most knowledgeable of all the people in that area with regard to these stories. Once he had become proficient in telling the stories, with the drawings, he travelled around from village to village and used the stories to bring the Christian message to these people. The response was very positive, and many of these people became Christians.

Singing/Chanting

Every nonliterate group has its own traditional songs as a very important part of their culture. For oral cultures, singing is not simply for entertainment, nor are songs only for special occasions, but rather singing is an integral part of the whole social structure. Singing is the oral expression that accompanies rituals and ceremonies, or it is just plain participation in events such as birth, puberty, initiation, harvesting, hunting, fishing, marriage, and death. It is also the medium used to celebrate victory in a battle, or to praise the people's great leaders, present and past. Some songs are used to recount traditional myths, legends, and moral codes. Singing also plays a most significant part in an oral culture's religious activities, being used in the praise and worship of deities, spirits, prophets, and ancestors, and in the many ceremonies and rituals associated with things such as healing from sickness, initiation, and exorcism of spirits (see Klem 1982, 126–56; Nicholls 1983, 50–64).

Bruce Olson relates how the Motilone Indians of Colombia, South America, used singing as the focus of their combined tribal get-togethers.

> Word spread that there was to be another Festival of the Arrows. There was excitement in the home. The festival was the only time all the Motilones gathered together.

> Pacts would be formed. Arrows would be exchanged, and the men forming the pact would have a singing contest. They would climb into their hammocks and sing as long as they could, relating legends, stories and news of recent events. Often their songs would last twelve hours, without interruption for food, water or rest. (Olson 1973, 152)

In many cases songs are stories set to music, and so they function in the same way as stories in being the oral storehouse of the people's history, religion, and cultural heritage. The added dimension of music makes the stories easier to remember and thus enables a much wider stratum of the community to possess and utilize the material than is evident with the more specialised storytelling skills.

It is unfortunate that the singing and chanting used in the Scriptures in their original presentation to an oral audience have not been preserved in some oral way for us. For people in Western, literacy-oriented societies, it would be most instructive to realize the considerable extent to which this communication form was employed by the people who first had the Scriptures presented to them. It is fascinating to try and imagine just how much Jesus himself sang and chanted the teachings he gave to his disciples; it is quite probable that it was a regular occurrence.

It is true that in contemporary Western society, sections of the Scriptures, such as the Psalms and many key passages of both Old and New Testaments, have been prepared in Western musical forms. But these are only a small percentage of the Scriptures that were originally used this way.

Poetry

Poetry is a significant form of communication in many nonliterate cultures, particularly in Middle Eastern ones. Historically, any important message to be communicated to the people was usually prepared in poetic form. For Muslim women in some countries, it was one of the few acceptable ways whereby they could make a protest and appeal for social justice and political reform.

> Women poets . . . used their works as a platform for involvement in the social currents of the day. Their poetry, for the most part topical and issue oriented, is to be valued more as a contribution to women's political awakening than for its intrinsic literary merit. These poems also provided the soil from which later works grew, works that will ultimately rank amongst the foremost and most valuable products of modern Persian poetry. (Fernea 1985, 317)

Poetry, as with storytelling and singing, is a communicational form used by oral cultures in the presentation and preservation of their cultural history and heritage. Instead of the special techniques that go with storytelling and the music that accompanies singing, poetry uses rhyme and rhythm, imagery and metaphor, assonance and alliteration, and many other oral techniques, to give a colourful presentation of its material, and also to provide a structure for memorization.

In Western, literacy-oriented cultures, poetry is often seen as a specialized literary skill, practised and appreciated by a limited group, and so its considerable communicational impact often remains unused. In Australia, for instance, many of the important values and ideals of the culture are enshrined in epic poems such as A. B. (Banjo) Paterson's "The Man from Snowy River" (1987, 1) and Dorothea MacKellar's "My Country" (1981, 1). These poems are well known by many Australians, but few of them would feel comfortable about reciting such a poem in public, or even in private with a group of friends. That sort of thing is left to the "specialists," the teachers of English literature and the professional actors.

In many oral cultures, however, poetry is accepted as a normal part of the people's cultural expression, and they delight in the way poetry uses their own language to provide colourful, emotional expression for their own cultural heritage, and for everyday experiences as well (see Klem 1982, 110–38; Nicholls 1983, 13–34). For people in such societies, it should not be difficult at all to identify with the messages and communication forms that Jesus used in the Gospels, or with other messages contained in the Scriptures, so many of which are poetic in form.

Drama/Dance

Drama is a very ancient part of the fabric of human society. For thousands of years people have used this art form to make dynamic presentations of traditional myths and legends, important historical events and battles, and contemporary parables that highlight traditional values and beliefs. In many cases the drama has a musical accompaniment, and other art forms such as poetry, singing, and dance are included as an integral part of the drama. This means that drama is often a multimedia performance. In oral cultures, because of their characteristic of participation, drama is often a very communal affair, with the audience becoming involved in various ways, such as with instrumental accompaniment, singing, or set spoken responses. Corroborees performed by the Australian Aborigines are a typical example of this, when the whole community is often able to become involved (Ollerenshaw 1986, 9).

Kath Nicholls talks about "Asian Theatre" and how India has strongly influenced the forms of drama throughout Asia. In spite of this pervasive Indian influence, there is an incredible variety of drama and dance throughout the Asian region. The Thai *ligay* drama, the Japanese *kabuki* plays, the Malaysian *wayang kulit* shadow plays, and the Balinese dances are just a few examples of how every area has its own distinctive drama forms (Nicholls 1983, 112–35).

In Papua New Guinea the dramatic enactment of traditional stories and rituals is done in the form of what are called "sing-sings." Except for some sacred rituals, the whole community usually participates in these. In some cases, preparations for these sing-sings may take many weeks, and the decorations worn by the participants, especially the headdresses, are very colourful and spectacular. The singing and dancing of these performances will often go right through the night until dawn. The participants will rest through the day and repeat the procedure during the next night. This is not the only form of drama used in Papua New Guinea, but probably the most distinctive one (McGregor 1982, 21–66).

These examples of drama and dance in contemporary oral societies form close parallels to those found in the Israelite Old Testament community.

Genealogies

Papua New Guinean people have a remarkable interest in genealogies. For them a genealogy is not simply a list of names, but an extremely important part of their heritage. It is their link with their ancestors, whom they believe to be present in the spiritual realm and exerting a strong influence on their lives and well-being. Many knowledgeable men can trace their ancestry back hundreds of years, and have many thousands of names in their memory (see Bateson 1958, 222–23).

The following is an account of one missionary translator's encounter with the significance of genealogies to the Papua New Guinean people.

When we began translating . . . we started on the book of Matthew. . . . We started translating at chapter one, verse eighteen, because we didn't want to translate chapter one, verses one to seventeen as they were the genealogies. I didn't want to put the people off a perfectly good book by starting at this dry uninteresting stuff. . . . When we finished the book of Matthew, we turned back to the genealogies. We translated from the passage, "Abraham begat Isaac, and Isaac begat Jacob and Jacob . . ." and we translated this last because we didn't want to put them off the book.

I wrote it out in pencil and that night I went up to the village where there was a meeting on. Someone said, "Well you better bring that with you." So I put it in my pocket, went up there and sat down in the house. Then I was asked, "Well, what have you got?" Now they all knew what I had because my language helper had told them what

I had and he was excited about it but he didn't tell me that. But all the people gathered round because it was something important that I had in my pocket.

So they said, "All right, sit down and read what you've got." I said, "Oh, it's just what we translated. . . ." "Read it and we'll hear and then we'll have our meeting" . . . . And so we read from the genealogies: and as I read down "Abraham begat Isaac, Isaac begat Jacob, . . ." the people began to move closer and closer. . . . [T]hey were all packed tightly around me. And as I read the air was tense. I didn't know what was going on—I was getting a little bit nervous—what were they going to do? And the elder of the village was sitting beside me and watched me read. . . . When I read the full stop at the end, he put his hand down like this and just about wiped the noses of the people in front of me—they were so close. He said, "Listen you people, listen. This is no myth or white man's fable. This is truth. What myth ever carefully writes down people's names down through history? None ever! This is the truth. This actually happened!" (Oatridge 1975)

So what was in one person's perspective something dry and uninteresting was the seal of absolute truth to others. This became a key factor in establishing the word of God among these Papua New Guinean people.

These people perceived something of the true significance of the genealogy in Matthew chapter 1. What about those of us who are literacy-oriented people? Have we perceived that significance—or is this a passage that we prefer to skim over? And what about all the other genealogies scattered throughout the Scriptures? Do Western Christians understand their relevance and significance? Oral communicators probably would!

PRESERVATION AND REMEMBERING OF ORAL INFORMATION

People in literate cultures are often amazed at the amounts of information that can be stored in the memories of oral peoples. While not taking anything away from the skill and intense mental effort required by people to carry out these feats of memory, the reason that literates are so amazed is usually because they misunderstand the way oral people preserve their information and expect that it is done in the same way that literates would do it.

Modern research has again brought fresh understanding to this subject and, while not detracting from the oral artists' skills and intelligence, removed some of the mystery. The following information from researchers in various fields will help to give us a more complete understanding of how this preservation and remembering process operates.

> Verbal memory skill is understandably a valued asset in oral cultures. But the way verbal memory works in oral art forms is quite different from what literates in the past commonly imagined. In a literate culture verbatim memorization is commonly done from a text, to which the memorizer returns as often as necessary to perfect and test verbatim mastery.
>
> In the past, literates have commonly assumed that oral memorization in an oral culture normally achieved the same goal of absolutely verbatim repetition. (Ong 1982, 57–63)

Ong describes how the research done by Milman Parry and Albert Lord has been significant in this area. Parry demonstrated that the works attributed to the great Greek poet Homer (c. 800 BC), such as the *Iliad* and the *Odyssey*, were basically oral creations. The composed verses, with their metrical rhythm, were made up of formulas. These formulas were groups of words that dealt specifically with traditional materials. Each formula was shaped to fit into a specific metrical rhythm. The poet had a massive vocabulary of these formulas with which he could fabricate correct metrical lines almost without limit.

> Parry tested this concept with contemporary Yugoslav narrative poets. . . . [T]heir narrative poems, like Homer's, were metric and formulaic. . . .
>
> Comparison of the recorded songs, however, reveals that, though metrically regular, they were never sung the same way twice. Basically the same formulas and themes recurred, but they were stitched together or "rhapsodized" differently in each rendition even by the same poet, depending on audience reaction, the mood of the poet or of the occasion, and other social and psychological factors. . . .

> A singer will protest that he can do his own version of a song line for line and word for word any time. . . . [W]hen, however, their purported verbatim renditions are recorded and compared, they turn out to be never the same, though the songs are recognizable versions of the same story. (Ibid.)

This helps us to understand that an oral person's concept of "line for line" and "word for word" is not quite the same as a literate person's text-oriented concept. So we find that there are variations in the accuracy of verbatim repetition of oral communications.

Two of the things that act as constraints to aid the verbatim repetition of oral works are music and ritual. Of interest to Christian communicators are Ong's comments on the ritual of the Eucharist:

> Ritual utterance itself is often not typically verbatim. "Do this in memory of me" Jesus said at the last supper (Luke 22:19). Christians celebrate the Eucharist as their central act of worship because of Jesus' directive. But the crucial words that Christians repeat as Jesus' words in fulfilling this directive (that is, the words "This is my body . . . ; this is the cup of my blood . . .") do not appear in exactly the same way in any two places where they are cited in the New Testament. The early Christian church remembered, in pretextual, oral form, even in her textualized rituals, and even at those very points where she was commanded to remember most assiduously. (Ibid., 65)

Another aspect of communication in oral cultures that is often linked with memorization is that of signs. Hand signs, gestures, and other kinds of body movement can all be used as aids to memory. This is an aspect of oral communication that is often overlooked by literates, largely because it cannot usually be written down. But to regard it as insignificant would be to make a major wrong assumption.

Melanesian people, who are still largely oral communicators, have gained a reputation for having prodigious memories, and some useful insights on this are presented in the book *Oral Tradition in Melanesia* by Donald Denoon and Rod Lacey (1981).

The clansman's memory gives him a grasp of the ancestral time, when all things had their origin. His memory is communal. It is the passing on of most sacred possessions from father to son. . . . [T]he elder regards his own history as universal, because his memory and the rites he practises tell him of his living continuity with his children and his ancestors who also live. (Antony Ruhan, in ibid., 41)

The techniques discussed are not mysterious or magical but are basically just ways of helping people to remember things. Accuracy is perceived quite differently from the way Western, text-oriented people perceive it, and depends on many things in the people's situation. Fixed texts are very uncommon in oral literature, and it is more probable that people will remember a number of slightly different versions of whatever they are learning. In this context of oral learning, it is important for the undistorted preservation of knowledge that the content and mode of presentation of the material be kept conservative.

Poetry is another memory device that is common in oral cultures:

Complex poetic techniques were developed in oral cultures and specialists in poetry have existed in a number of different cultures. Navigators on Puluwat use poetic devices to help remember information about star courses between islands and seamarks on the course.

Other mnemonic devices depend on matching the key words to be remembered with a story or legend or other set of words known off by heart by the learner. This technique was used by Gilbertese navigators to help remember star directions for voyages. Stories about the various stars or constellations needed for finding direction are used to assist the navigator's memory of the order of the different directions to be followed.

Man-made objects such as paintings, buildings, tombs, and models can be used to visualize things which it is desired to remember. . . . Human performance in dance, music, or ritual can also serve as a means of storing or recalling knowledge.

Pebbles or stones are used in the Caroline Islands to teach the comparative positions of the main points of the Caroline star compass. They are also used to illustrate the way in which navigators can keep track of where they are on ocean voyages.

Many other examples could be added. It should be clear from these examples that oral cultures have available to them a wide variety of methods which could be used for transmitting knowledge with some accuracy. (Lyndsay Farrall, in ibid., 71–87)

Paul Muench, who also based his research on experience in Melanesia, describes how significant memorization processes are in relation to the preservation of the history of a people. He lists storytelling, poetry, songs, symbols, rituals, and drama as some of the major communication forms used by oral people in the preservation of their own history and culture (1984).

Storytelling is used by many people, but some are much better storytellers than others. The rules for storytelling are not well defined, and there is no formal training, but an outsider who assumes that the form is the same as that in the outsider's culture is making a very wrong assumption and will inevitably produce poor communication.

Where an event is produced in the form of poetry, it has a much better chance of survival as history, because it is easier for the whole community to remember it. The beauty of the poetic form and the power of its symbolism help people to remember not only the event but also the emotions associated with it.

Songs have all the qualities of poetry but add the benefit of music as another memory aid. Songs are very often linked with drama or rituals or symbols, or various combinations of them, and all these forms reinforce each other as means of preserving oral history.

Cave paintings, roll call sticks, knotted strings, pictures, sculptures, and buildings are other forms that Muench mentions as being used to help people remember events or persons in their history.

Oral history by its very nature is more a community product. The effort of transmitting oral history requires more people. With the involvement of more people, there is more participation in the composition. Also, because oral history requires an audience and because the performer gets direct and immediate feedback from the audience, oral history is more easily and quickly adapted to the needs and desires of the audience. Written history is not as flexible as oral history.

The methods used by a people to aid memory will have an impact on how those people remember. History is influenced by the methods of doing history. (Ibid., 135–54)

The information outlined above shows how the oral system of preserving and remembering important information is very different from the literacy-oriented system. We must recognize that each one is much more appropriate in the correspondingly appropriate context.

ORAL PEOPLE'S RESISTANCE TO LITERACY

Klem carried out a study of oral communication based on the African context. Klem's study was motivated by the "problem" in Africa that after more than a century of mission and government efforts to bring literacy and Western education to the African people, a large percentage of people were still nonliterate, and many of this group seemed resistant not only to literacy but also to the Christian gospel. Klem carried out research among this group in order to try and identify the reason(s) for this problem.

In order to probe the problems . . . it was found necessary to study the communication systems indigenous to West Africa. . . . The non-reading masses of Yorubaland and much of West Africa are oral communicators. They are usually illiterate only by Western standards, since they give great attention to the preservation and transmission of oral literature. It is not that they do not learn, teach or communicate. It is that we from the West do not appreciate a system based on oral (rather than written) communication and memorization as is customary in an indigenous African setting. There was and is an indigenous communication system perfectly capable of being used to communicate the gospel effectively to the majority of the people. They do not have to learn a new method of communicating. (1982, xviii)

These research findings give us a glimpse into the wide range of communication skills used by oral communicators and help us to understand that their system is a very comprehensive one indeed. Klem's statement points to a key issue in determining an effective strategy for communicating the Christian message to oral people: Do we recognize that oral communicators have a wide variety of skills and a communication system that is completely adequate to receive the Christian message? Or do we, as do many in cross-cultural ministry, feel that the only way to effectively communicate Christianity is to teach people our Western, literacy-oriented system?

The research findings given above, and the remarkable variety of oral communication skills that have been described, should help us to understand why Jesus himself used the communication techniques he did in order that his disciples, and his wider audience, could understand and remember his teaching. It also helps us to understand why he didn't use books and literacy.

CONCLUSION

There are several very important points for us to learn from these past two chapters. Firstly, there are oral communicators in the world today, and not a few; in fact, the majority of the world's population can be classified as such. Secondly, oral communicators are highly skilled people who operate within a sophisticated system of communication. Finally, their communicational skills are demonstrated through an incredible variety of dynamic and exciting forms that make most literate communities pale by comparison. This is especially so when we consider the percentages of the oral and literate communities that actually participate in their respective communicational forms.

It is important for us to realize that the communication skills of oral people, such as those described above, are not simply "spare-time" hobbies or leisure activities. They are the characteristics of an oral society—a part of the basic framework of that society. As such they cannot be ignored or put aside as unimportant when we consider appropriate strategies for communicating the Christian message to oral people.

These facts merit our serious and very thorough consideration if we are concerned at all about effective communication of the Christian message to oral peoples. It is therefore appropriate for us now to move on and consider some of the examples from the Scriptures of how the word of God was communicated to oral people. We may not have considered the Scriptures in that context before, and in particular how Jesus himself communicated his message to an oral community. So this could be both a revelation and a challenge to us as we consider the possibility of our own ministry in a similar context.

3

WHY DIDN'T JESUS WRITE A BOOK? THE MINISTRY OF JESUS TO AN ORAL, EVENT-ORIENTED COMMUNITY

This chapter focuses on the ministry of Jesus to an oral, event-oriented community. The purpose of this study is to reinforce the proposition which is the underlying theme of this book. The proposition states that for people who are oral communicators, the oral communication techniques of their own culture are the most appropriate ones to use, for both the communication of Christian truths to them and for the training of their Christian leadership. This is a general, all-inclusive statement, but as we examine the ministry of Jesus this statement becomes much more specific, for we discover that Jesus' messages in the Gospels were all prepared for oral communicators and presented to them by means of appropriate oral communication forms. This example of Jesus provides us with an excellent model for anyone considering development of a strategy for communicating God's word to oral societies. We may not have considered Jesus' ministry in this way before, but as we examine the Gospels we will see just how relevant his ministry is in the context of Christian communication to oral people.

THE GALILEAN CONTEXT OF JESUS' MINISTRY

The casual reader of the Gospels would probably not be aware that a large portion of the early ministry of Jesus was spent in Galilee, an area some four or five days' journey north of Jerusalem. People may recognize names of areas such as Judea and Samaria, and places like Bethany, Nazareth, and Capernaum, but not realize that there was any significance as to whether Jesus was in one place or another. However, if we start to ask questions such as "Where did Jesus conduct his early ministry?" and "Who were the people in his audience?" we find some rather startling answers.

The answers to "Where?" and "Who?" are, for the most part, Galilee and Galileans. In fact, if Mark were the only Gospel we read, it would appear that following Jesus' baptism and temptation, he ministered exclusively in the region of Galilee until he began his final journey to Jerusalem. The other Gospels do give us details of other places he visited during that time. John in particular gives some detailed information about Jesus' visits to Jerusalem, but it is still clear that the majority of his time was spent in Galilee. Why would Jesus want to spend so much of his time there? As we look closely at the history of Galilee, it seems unlikely that the long-promised Jewish Messiah would indeed want to spend most of his time in that territory.

The area of Galilee had a turbulent history, right from the time the Israelites, under the leadership of Joshua, entered and claimed that territory in the name of Jehovah. Many Canaanite people remained in the land, and for a long period of time it was strongly influenced by pagan nations all around it. Then came the Assyrian conquest (c. 722 BC), and many of the Jewish people were deported to other countries and replaced by foreigners. The small number of Jews who had remained there were still proud of their heritage, but it was inevitable that because of their intermixing with other peoples their religious and cultural convictions would be weakened.

Many years later, after the return of the southern Jews from exile in Babylon (c. 538–516 BC), the northern Jews were regarded as not being pure Hebrew stock and so were despised by the southerners. Later on, during Maccabean times (167–160 BC), Galilee was the scene of fighting between Jews and the Seleucid Empire, and those recognised as genuine Jews relocated around Jerusalem. Galilee was left as a heathen land. Then under John Hyrcanus (135–104 BC) the Jewish state began to expand again, and Galilee was reconquered. The people there were given the choice of expulsion or converting to Judaism; many chose the latter and soon merged with the Jewish people. Synagogues and schools were established to teach new converts.

The resultant Jewish people that emerged from this turbulent history to be present in Galilee at the time of Christ had developed their own regional brand of Judaism with their own customs and strong sense of independence. They were surrounded by people of other cultures and under strong Hellenistic influences, especially during the rule of Herod the Great. Edersheim gives us some helpful details of how Galilee and Galileans were viewed by Palestinians in the time of Christ:

> Greater contrast could scarcely be imagined than between the intricate scholastic studies of the Judeans, and the active pursuits that engaged men in Galilee. It was a common saying: "If a person wishes to be rich, let him go north; if he wants to be wise, let him come south"—and to Judea, accordingly, flocked, from ploughshare and workshop, whoever wished to become "learned in the Law." The very neighbourhood of the Gentile world, the contact with the great commercial centres close by, and the constant intercourse with foreigners, who passed through Galilee along one of the world's great highways, would render the narrow exclusiveness of the Southerners impossible. Galilee was to Judaism "the Court of the Gentiles"—the Rabbinic Schools of Judea its innermost Sanctuary.

> In religious observances their practice was simpler; as regarded canon-law they often took independent views, and generally followed the interpretations of those who . . . inclined to the more mild and rational—we had almost said, the more human—application of traditionalism. . . . There was a general contempt in Rabbinic circles for all that was Galilean. Although the Judean or Jerusalem dialect was far from pure, the people of Galilee were especially blamed for neglecting the study of their language, charged with errors in grammar, and especially with absurd malpronunciation, sometimes leading to ridiculous mistakes.

> Among such a people, and in that country, Jesus spent by far the longest part of his life upon earth. (1962, vol. 1, 223–26)

In other words, Galilee was really not the place where the Jews would have expected the Messiah to conduct his ministry. To them, Jerusalem and Judea were much more appropriate locations. The temple was there, the Jewish religious leaders lived there, and that was the "correct" place for the discussion and presentation of important religious matters. This was no doubt part of the reason why Jesus encountered so much opposition from the Jewish leaders (Mark 3:22; John 7:47–52). By concentrating his ministry in Galilee, Jesus had in effect rejected the Jewish religious leaders and their strict legalistic practices. He chose to put his new wine into Galilean wineskins! This meant teaching his disciples and the common people in their own heart language of Aramaic, and by means of the oral communication forms and techniques with which they were familiar.

Galilee was a reasonably prosperous farming and fishing community. Numerous roads passed through the area and brought trade—mainly with Gentiles. The common language was Aramaic, but Greek was widely used for commercial purposes. Latin was the language of the occupying Roman legions, and so was also reasonably well known, and Hebrew was used among the learned rabbis.

These Galileans were not as religiously conservative as their southern Jewish counterparts, and their historical background and present circumstances meant that they also had a much broader outlook on life in general. In addition, they had a greater tolerance of the non-Jewish people around them. This gives us part of the answer as to why Jesus spent most of his time there. The message that Jesus taught emphasised a genuine heart worship of God rather than an outward observance of ceremonies, rituals, and Sabbath keeping, and he focused on people loving their neighbour through practical ways of caring and giving rather than by a legalistic observance of the Jewish law (see Matt 5–7; 12:1–14). The Galileans were much more likely to be receptive to a new and innovative message such as this one that Jesus brought to them.

THE GALILEAN RESPONSE TO JESUS' MINISTRY

As we turn to the terse and often fast-paced style of Mark's Gospel, it is not difficult to sense the enthusiasm of the response of the Galileans to Jesus' message and ministry. The following are some brief examples:

They went to Capernaum, and when the Sabbath came, Jesus went into the synagogue and began to teach. The people were amazed at his teaching, because he taught them as one who had authority, not as the teachers of the law. Just then a man in their synagogue who was possessed by an impure spirit cried out, "What do you want with us, Jesus of Nazareth? Have you come to destroy us? I know who you are—the Holy One of God!"

"Be quiet!" said Jesus sternly. "Come out of him!" The impure spirit shook the man violently and came out of him with a shriek.

The people were all so amazed that they asked each other, "What is this? A new teaching—and with authority! He even gives orders to impure spirits and they obey him." News about him spread quickly over the whole region of Galilee. (Mark 1:21–28,)

A few days later, when Jesus again entered Capernaum, the people heard that he had come home. They gathered in such large numbers that there was no room left, not even outside the door, and he preached the word to them. (Mark 2:1,2;)

When they had crossed over, they landed at Gennesaret and anchored there. As soon as they got out of the boat, people recognized Jesus. They ran throughout that whole region and carried the sick on mats to wherever they heard he was. And everywhere he went—into villages, towns or countryside—they placed the sick in the marketplaces. They begged him to let them touch even the edge of his cloak, and all who touched it were healed. (Mark 6:53–56)

So there is little doubt that the Galilean people responded in a very positive way to Jesus. And even though his message and methods were new and innovative, they were eager to accept him.

THE PEOPLE IN JESUS' AUDIENCE

Now that we understand where Jesus spent most of his time, it is also important for us to know exactly who these people were that were in his audience. Apart from his close disciples, the audience is identified not as the religious leaders, or influential people, but the common people of Galilee. These were the ones referred to derisively as the *amhaares*, the "people of the land," by the Jewish upper class.

> He chose to consort with the "amhaares," the "people of the land"—
> tax collectors and other bad company, who were treated by the
> Pharisees as beyond the pale of true religion, for whom no hope of
> salvation is possible (Luke 15:1, John 7:49). Further, he even called
> one of them to be his disciple. The position of publicans in Roman-
> occupied Palestine was particularly obnoxious to the loyal Jews,
> smacking of compromise with the hated invaders and affording an
> opportunity for extortion and fraud. (Martin 1975, 182)

But these were the people to whom Jesus came to minister, and their enthusiastic response was part of the reason that Jesus came to them. The other reason was that, just as the Galileans were the people most prepared to respond to Jesus, so, of all the Jewish people in Palestine at that time, they were the people most prepared to take the message of Jesus and pass it on to others, especially Gentile people.

The Apostle Peter is probably a prime example of what the Galileans were like. He was fiercely independent, and yet prepared to forsake his own prosperous livelihood and commit himself to a new, charismatic religious leader. He was also the sort of person who was not fastidious about Jewish hand-washing rituals. He was betrayed by his Galilean accent when he denied any knowledge of Jesus, but later on, as leader of the new group of Christ's followers, he stood firm against the opposition of the conservative southern Jewish authorities.

And it was Peter who was chosen to break new ground with the message of the gospel to the Gentiles. He was already involved in taking the message to new places and people in Palestine, and was staying in the house of a tanner, normally regarded as "unclean" by the Jews. There the Holy Spirit commissioned him to go to the home of Cornelius, a Gentile centurion. This was not an easy task, even for Peter, but eventually he was able to put aside his traditional Jewish dislike of Gentiles, minister to them in their own home, and then take the unprecedented step of baptising non-Jewish people and declaring that they were right with God—without having to first become Jews (Acts 9:43–10:48)!

So it was the Galilean common people, like Peter, with whom Jesus spent his time; in fact he seemed to delight in associating with the nonreligious types of people, such as tax collectors. These were people who were definitely "not approved" by the religious leaders, but were obviously very important to Jesus. He even made one of them, Matthew, into a disciple.

Jesus also had a significant ministry to women, who in the Jewish society of that time were often regarded as second-class citizens. Jesus treated them with honour and respect and gave quality time to them in his teaching ministry (Luke 10:38–41).

Jesus maintained a lively dialogue with the Jewish religious leaders, who in many cases travelled all the way from Jerusalem to Galilee just to investigate the stories they had heard of this remarkable man and his teachings (Mark 7:1–15).

This all may seem rather strange to us, because in our understanding of biblical matters Jerusalem was the religious capital of the people and the obvious centre for proclaiming any new development of Judaism, especially if it called for Jesus to make a proclamation, or take some action as the Messiah. But as we consider the whole context of Galilee, its history and inhabitants, it helps us to understand why this was the place Jesus preferred to be. It also helps us to understand why Galileans responded so positively to Christ and his message, and then were instrumental in spreading it far and wide during the early days of the church.

JESUS' COMMUNICATION PROGRAM IN GALILEE

So we can see that the audience and the location were chosen by Jesus for special reasons:

1. The Galilean people were not as religiously conservative as those in Judea and Jerusalem, and so were much more likely to be open to receive him and his message, with its new and innovative teaching.
2. In the context of Galilee, there was a much greater opportunity for Jesus to bring his message to all levels of society, rather than in the class-conscious society of Jerusalem.
3. When the time came, the Galilean people were more likely to be ready to take Jesus' message "into all the world, and preach the Good News to everyone, everywhere" (Mark 16:15 TLB)—including Gentiles and Samaritans.

Even more important than that, there were special reasons why Jesus was the sort of communicator he was, and why he used the communication techniques he used. It wasn't simply the message he brought, although that was special too, but *how* he communicated that message that gave it such dynamic impact.

ORAL COMMUNICATION IN THE TIME OF JESUS

The Aramaic, Greek, Latin, and Hebrew languages were all used to a greater or lesser extent in Galilee during the time of Jesus. Aramaic was the common language, and the majority of the people understood this. However, it was a language that was mainly used orally, and there were few written Aramaic materials available. The Jewish religious leaders forbade any of the Scriptures (i.e., Old Testament) to be translated and written down in Aramaic. They insisted that this could only be done in Hebrew, although they did tolerate the Greek Septuagint translation.

Hebrew was the religious language of the Jewish people. It was taught in the synagogue schools, and the Hebrew Scriptures were read (and translated) there to the people each Sabbath day. However, most of the teaching of Hebrew was done orally, by chanting the Scriptures. In spite of the educational institutions that were available, no more than 5 percent of the population had reached the stage that we would classify as functionally literate in Hebrew. Greek was the language of commerce and trade, and again was mostly used orally, although a certain amount of Greek literature was available for those who could read it. Latin was the language of the occupying Roman forces, but its use was limited and was probably restricted mainly to internal military and administrative matters (see Klem 1982, 61–74, for a comprehensive treatment of the linguistic context of Palestine at the time of Christ).

From the evidence we have, oral communication was by far the most dominant means of communication in the Galilean community.

> Apart from the main centres of culture like Athens and Rome, the first half of the first Christian century was still a non-literary age. It is hard to think oneself out of a situation in which, if a man has something to say, he naturally writes a book. The days of printing and of mass circulation lay still many centuries ahead. The writing of books was not then the natural and inevitable procedure that it is now.

This was particularly true of Jewish society. The great mass of Jewish law and tradition was passed down by word of mouth. The teaching of the rabbis was oral. The Mishnah is the codified summary of the Jewish law, and it was not put into writing until the third century AD. According to Jewish standards, a good student was not a great reader, because there were no books to read, but a good listener, and a good rememberer who was like "a well plastered cistern which never loses a drop of water." The reverence which a Jewish scholar accorded to the scriptures of the Old Testament made him utterly unwilling himself to put anything into writing, lest he might appear to be putting his productions on a level with the sacred and the holy writings. "Commit nothing to writing," was the rabbinic maxim. (Barclay 1975, 24)

This may help us to understand that the general attitude of the people of that era towards oral communication was completely different from that which we find in Western society today, where the emphasis is so strongly on literacy and books. To them the oral message was authoritative, important, and much preferred to the written message. It represented a process of careful learning and interpretation and, being embodied in a living person, was much more highly valued than "dead" words written on paper.

JESUS' IDENTITY AS A COMMUNICATOR

The evidence of the Gospels and the testimony of history leave us in no doubt that Jesus was a brilliant communicator. However, it is important that we realize that Jesus was a communicator in the context of the oral society in which he lived. He should not be perceived in terms of a Western, literacy-oriented communicator, living in a literacy-oriented society, with all that that entails. He was an oral communicator, in an oral society, and he identified himself very clearly as such.

Jesus as a Teacher

Jesus set out at the beginning of his public ministry to declare himself as a teacher. In Luke 4:16–21 we have the account of the event in the synagogue at Nazareth when Jesus declared himself as the fulfilment of the messianic prophecy. In doing this, Jesus was following the traditional religious culture of the Israelites, and yet at the same time he was being very innovative. He had not received training from any of the recognised teachers of his time, as was the acceptable procedure for aspiring teachers. Instead he chose his own methods of teaching and his own interpretation of the Old Testament Scriptures.

Jesus was regarded as a teacher by his disciples, and also by the common people, even though they recognised that he was a very different kind of teacher. In order for Jesus to become an accredited teacher, recognised by the contemporary scholarly community, he would have had to become a disciple in one of the established rabbinic schools, yet he chose not to do so. Although Jesus lacked accreditation from any of the established rabbinic schools, he was still very much a teacher in the true sense, and there is plenty of testimony to justify this claim. The Gospels make it very clear that Jesus was regarded as a respected teacher by his own disciples, by Jewish leaders such as Nicodemus, by other Jewish teachers, and by the common people (Mark 10:51; Luke 10:25; 18:18; John 1:38; 3:2).

So Jesus deliberately took the role of a teacher, but a very different kind of teacher— one who was interested mostly in teaching the common people. For this reason he apparently did not teach through the scholarly languages of Greek and Hebrew, but chose the common language, Aramaic. Jesus knew what modern research has confirmed: that if you want to have maximum communicational impact with a message, it must be communicated in the heart language of the hearers (Dye 1985, 103–6; McGavran 1980, 217–20). Aramaic was the language of the home, the countryside, and the only language in which the vast majority felt truly at ease. This is the language Jesus used. "Dalman gives extensive evidence from the traces of Aramaic in the Greek texts of the Gospels that Jesus probably taught and ministered in the mother tongue of the majority of the common people" (Klem 1982, 70; see also Dalman 1929, 7–18; Black 1967).

Jesus chose to have an itinerant teaching ministry among the peasants, and took his disciples out into the countryside, by the seashore, and through the hamlets and villages. Jesus' teaching program was nonformal and unstructured, but at the same time it was a highly intensive, twenty-four-hours-a-day program. Some of Jesus' disciples, such as Matthew and John, were literate, but the majority were probably not. So Jesus' teaching program was prepared so that all could learn and participate. Jesus conducted his leadership training program without the aid of any books or literacy classes, yet at the end of three short and turbulent years he was able to leave these young leaders, fully confident that they would be able to carry out the task that he assigned to them. Jesus' prayer for his disciples in John 17:1–26 takes on remarkable significance in this respect as he says, "I gave them the words you gave me and they accepted them" (v. 8), and "I have given them your word and the world has hated them" (v. 14). Jesus was confident that his disciples had received the message he had come to give them, and that they would be able to pass it on to others—yet there is no evidence that he left any of that message in written form.

In stating the above I do not want to diminish in any way the fact that the disciples were able to achieve their remarkable success in evangelism and church planting through the power of the Holy Spirit, who came to indwell them at Pentecost. However, there is no evidence to suggest that the message they proclaimed and taught was given to them in some miraculous way. Rather it was the result of the effective oral communication teaching program of Jesus and the oral communication skills of his disciples.

In his role as a teacher, Jesus sought to win a hearing as a human being rather than as a stereotyped teacher, healer, and saviour. As a result, he was accepted by many of the people with whom he identified, but rejected by some who could not accept him in this role.

Jesus as a Poet

Much of Jesus' teaching was presented in Aramaic poetic style, which uses parallelism, rhythm, assonance, imagery, and rhyme. In other words, he didn't just stand up and preach a long message each time he taught something important. Careful preparation was made of stories, parables, and other teaching, and these were presented in poetic form so they could be memorized and then transmitted to others through the same oral system.

> Burney was among the first to demonstrate that when the words of Jesus as recorded in our present Gospels are translated back into Aramaic, they fall into rather balanced and rhythmic lines of Aramaic poetry. The lines are complete with assonance, rhythm, not infrequently rhyme (1925, 147).

A few other rabbis were known to give some of their sayings in rhythmic form, but in the consistent use of poetic structures, and particularly rhyme and elaborated parables, the teachings of Jesus are unique (Burney 1925, 148; Jeremias 1971, 29).

Jeremias is among those scholars who claim that the use of parables, creative figures of speech and structures of Hebrew folk culture are distinctive marks of the work of Jesus, Ipsissima Vox, "His very words" (1971, 29; Burney 1925, 6f). In this regard he follows Dalman. He further claims that our Lord, in His role as a rabbi, was expected to drill His students to memorize His words, so that they would not pass from memory (Jeremias 1971, 20; Manson 1948, 12ff; V. Taylor 1933, 94). When Christ did this in Aramaic oral-poetic style, the common people could participate. (Klem 1982, 78)

Barclay, in referring to the sayings of Jesus, has some comments to make about Jesus' use of poetry. He says that we should remember that in Jesus' time the printed book did not exist, and that a teacher would be failing in his objective if he didn't make his material memorable, as his students could not possess it any other way. He gives us the following examples:

(a) Much of the material is poetic in form. Hebrew poetry does not have rhyme, but it does have rhythm. Take a passage like Matthew 6:25–26. We give it in the Moffatt version, for Moffatt prints it as poetry.

> Therefore I tell you,
>> never trouble about what you are to eat or drink in life,
>> or about what you are to put on your body;
> surely life means more than food,
>> surely the body means more than clothes!
> Look at the wild birds;
>> they sow not, they reap not, they gather nothing in granaries,
>> and yet your heavenly Father feeds them.
> Are you not worth more than birds?

That is poetry designed to lodge in the memory.

(b) Jesus used patterns, made all the more memorable by repetition and reiteration. If we take a passage like Matthew 5:17–22 (NEB), and strip it of all the additional and incidental material, we get a pattern like this:

> Do not suppose that I have come to abolish the Law and the prophets;
> I did not come to abolish, but to complete . . .

> You have learned that our forefathers were told,
>   Do not commit murder;
> Anyone who commits murder
>   must be brought to judgment,
> But what I tell you is this:
>   Anyone who nurses anger against his brother
>   must be brought to judgment.

> You have learned that they were told,
>   Do not commit adultery;
> But what I tell you is this,
>   If a man looks at a woman with a lustful eye,
>   he has already committed adultery with her in his heart.

The pattern and the reiteration are clear.
In a passage like Luke 6:32–35 (NEB) the rhythmic pattern is even clearer:

> If you love only those who love you,
>   what credit is that to you?
>   Even sinners love those who love them.

> If you do good to those who do good to you,
>   what credit is that to you?
>   Even sinners do as much.

The rhythmic verse pattern is clear and memorable.

(c) Parallelism is characteristic of Hebrew style. The Hebrew writers tended to say everything twice, restating, developing, amplifying the statement first made. There are three types of this parallelism in Hebrew style and all are exemplified in the Gospel account of the teaching of Jesus.

There is synonymous parallelism, in which the second line reiterates the first.

> Is it permitted on the Sabbath
>> To do good or to do evil,
>> To save life or to destroy it? (Luke 6:9)

There is antithetical parallelism, in which the second line contrasts with the first.

> The Sabbath was made for man,
> Not man for the Sabbath (Mark 2:27)

There is synthetic parallelism, in which the thought continues in a series of parallel lines.

> They go about with broad phylacteries,
>> And wear deep fringes on their robes,
> They like to have places of honour at feasts,
>> And chief seats in synagogues,
> To be greeted respectfully in the street,
>> And to be addressed as Rabbi (Matt. 23:5–7 NEB)

Rhythm is accentuated by making not only the whole lines, but also the phrases within the lines correspond.

> Give not
>> the holy thing
>>> to the dogs,
> And cast not
>> your pearls
>>> before swine (Matt. 7:6). (Barclay 1975, 43–45)

Poetry was the logical and culturally appropriate method for Jesus to use in teaching his disciples. It enabled them to memorize with comparative ease the new and extensive teaching he was presenting. It also meant that the crowds of common people who gathered to hear him in the open air, or the synagogues, could participate in and respond to this learning experience. In this way the reception and transmission of Jesus' message was not limited to the scholarly elite, but was given to the oral communicators, which also included the scholars. This then allowed for rapid communication of his message across the land and to all strata of society. "He communicated through life, oral artistry and ritual rather than by writing. He wrote no books yet he said, 'Heaven and earth will pass away, but my words will not pass away' (Matt. 24:35)" (Klem 1982, 81).

The "oral artistry" mentioned by Klem would include Jesus' incredible skill as a storyteller and his use of parables, which were usually associated with something familiar, like wheat (Matt 13:2–23), sheep (Luke 15:4–7), or an oil lamp (Matt 5:14–16), and which would conjure up an instant mental picture in the minds of the hearers. Jesus also showed a skillful use of dialogue with individuals (John 4:7–26), with his disciples (Mark 10:23–31), with the Jewish leaders (Luke 20:27–44), and with the crowds (John 6:25–59).

JESUS' TECHNIQUES: EFFECTIVE IN COMMUNICATION AND TRAINING

The Gospels give us brief but eloquent testimonies of the effectiveness of Jesus' communication techniques. Comments made such as "No one ever spoke the way this man does" (John 7:46) help us to see that Jesus was "no ordinary preacher," and the vast crowds that gathered to hear him didn't only come to see the spectacular miracles, but to listen to a message that spoke clearly and meaningfully to each one of them.

In commenting on the skill and effectiveness of Jesus as a communicator, we should also note the brilliance of his communicational strategy. He chose the oral communication system of his day so that his teaching was not restricted to the scholarly elite, but his methods ensured that everyone could learn. Not only that, his methods also ensured that everyone could teach.

Jesus used a discipleship model for training and had no restrictions on who might become a disciple, apart from the universal demand of total commitment to himself as Lord. Jesus included women among his disciples, as well as spiritual outcasts such as publicans and tax collectors. This meant that when these disciples began to spread the gospel, it moved with tremendous impetus, transmitted through an oral system and reaching to every level of society.

It is extremely interesting to examine the passage in Acts 4:5–13, where the Galileans, Peter and John, address the Jewish council. This council, which contained the scholarly elite of that time, was astonished at the confidence and ability that Peter and John displayed. These learned men were not likely to be impressed with anything less than people who demonstrated outstanding ability in the knowledge and interpretation of Scripture orally. They took particular note of the following with regard to Peter and John:

a. Peter and John were uneducated—that is, they had not been trained in any of the recognised rabbinic schools.

b. They were from among the common people, the *amhaares*, and so were not expected to know much more than the basic essentials of the Jewish religious law.

c. They recognised that they were imitating the teaching method of Jesus. No doubt a number of the council had heard Jesus speak and were aware of the content and techniques that he employed.

In other words, Jesus had used an oral communication technique to train his disciples, which, although culturally very relevant, was still quite a departure from the normally acceptable training programs of this kind. He had been able to include common people in his program without requiring any prerequisites other than total commitment to himself. And yet he succeeded in producing disciples who impressed the leading scholars of the land. These disciples were then using the same techniques to train others, and the result was a rapidly expanding movement.

CONCLUSION

So Jesus didn't write a book. To present his message of eternal life to the world, Jesus deliberately chose the oral communication system of the common people in preference to a literacy-oriented system such as that used by the Pharisees. The reasons for Jesus' choice can be summarized in this way:

a. Jesus' message could be communicated clearly and effectively to all levels of the oral society in which he lived.

b. Jesus' message could be learned by everyone and transmitted to others in the informal context of everyday living. People did not need to have specialized training or skills to be able to do this.

c. In an oral community such as that to which Jesus belonged, a person's message is closely identified with the person. Jesus' message was identified in this way with himself and indeed focused directly upon him. In the same way, Jesus wanted his message and himself to be identified with living people rather than with a written document. His disciples were to be living epistles (2 Cor 3:2,3).

d. In the situation of the people, places, and appropriate communication forms of his day, for Jesus to write a book which summarized his teachings or to instruct his disciples to do so would have meant a complete change in his communication procedure and strategy. The focus of his teaching would have changed from being nonformal, participatory, and oral, to being literary, or book-oriented, formal, and accessible to only a small percentage of the community.

e. There were economic reasons that made it impractical for Jesus to consider using a book and a formal, literacy-oriented program as the basis for an ongoing, relevant teaching program.

> We may suppose that some people could read or chant the Scriptures but few people had books in their homes. Most of the use of Scriptures in the homes was done from memory. Christ could not think of reaching the masses with a new message in His century through books in Hebrew or any language. Barclay estimates that at the beginning of the fourth century the cost of having a scribe make a copy of the four Gospels would be about 91 British pounds [Barclay 1966, 45]. That is nearly U.S.$300. Similar costs in Christ's time would have prevented most people from being able to read our Lord's teachings. (Klem 1982, 67)

So it is not difficult to understand why Jesus chose a much more dynamic and effective means to deliver and to spread abroad his message for all people: he used the oral communication system of the people. As we move on now and examine carefully the Scriptures of the Old Testament, we find that Jesus' communication techniques and strategy are given considerable support by them. This is for the simple reason that the audiences in most cases were also primarily oral people.

4

THE ORIGINAL PRESENTATION OF THE OLD TESTAMENT SCRIPTURES

The Old Testament is a remarkable collection of writings which I believe to be inspired by the Holy Spirit and therefore to be the very word of God. Nevertheless, even a brief glance through the Scriptures indicates clearly that there are many different forms and styles of communication contained there. It is not simply one person's thoughts and expressions, but those of many people. Gordis says it well:

> The Bible is a library of masterpieces written by men who are artists, not for art's sake, a conception which they would not have favoured had they known it, but for life's sake. They were impelled by a single purpose, to tell their message as directly and effectively as possible. With the sure instinct of genius, they utilized the literary techniques and forms of their day and developed them to perfection. Unbeknown to themselves, they produced a gallery of classics in which deceptive simplicity conceals the highest art. (1971, 42)

Yet these masterpieces, acclaimed by some of the greatest literary minds as unsurpassed in the field of literature, have an incredible unity, a remarkable thread of theme and story that links the first message and the last, and all others in between. This is the work of the Holy Spirit, guiding and superintending the whole process of presentation, preservation, and recognition of the message until we have now a complete book, or collection of books, that bears the unmistakable imprint of divine inspiration. It is "the Divine Word in human words" (Jewett 1988), and it is the significance of these human words on which I will now focus.

THE OLD TESTAMENT PEOPLES AND THEIR CULTURAL CONTEXT

When we consider the term "Old Testament peoples," we are thinking about people who lived in a number of differing cultural environments, spread over many hundreds of years. But still, in spite of the many cultural changes that occurred during those years, there were certain constants, and these constants are very important to our understanding of the significance of the original presentation of God's message to the Israelites.

One of these constants was the fact that the people were oral communicators. That is, only a small percentage were literate, and so almost all communication was done orally. Israelite society included a variety of oral communicational forms, and certain skills were needed in order to be able to use them. Again, it must be stressed that when people from literate societies regard oral communicators as ignorant and unskilled, this is far from the truth. One of the great skills involved in oral societies is the use of the memory. Some examples of this might help to underline the importance of understanding what these people were really like and, in particular, what they could do.

One example is from Melanesia. In 1936 an anthropologist, Gregory Bateson, did a study of the Iatmul people of the Sepik River (Papua New Guinea), and made the statement that these people were very skilled in the art of debating, particularly about names, genealogies, and totems. He estimated that a learned man among them would carry in his memory anything from ten to twenty thousand names (1958, 126)!

The situation in the Middle East and among certain demographics in Europe has historically been the same.

> Such a love of oral tradition, and of the memory which naturally goes with it, has been maintained in the East down to the present day: even an uneducated but practising Arab will easily know the Koran off by heart, and before the Nazi extermination of the Jews in Eastern Europe it was easy to find people, often in menial

occupations, who knew off by heart not only the whole of the Old Testament, but a large part of the Talmud. (Soggin 1976, 61)

So when we speak of the Old Testament peoples as being oral communicators, we are thinking of highly articulate people who were part of a rich culture that had a wide variety of oral communicational forms. Another constant for these people was the fact that their orientation was spiritual rather than secular. That is, their religious beliefs and spiritual concepts were not reserved for certain days or special rituals, but were an integral part of daily living. The gaining of their daily livelihood; the social context of birth, marriage, death, and community activities; their national events of war and celebration, as well as their regular religious observances, were all related directly to their worship of God. Naturally they expressed themselves about these matters and responded to God's dealings with them as a people through their oral communication forms. But this meant that they presented not only historical and cultural materials in these communications, but also their faith in and understanding of God. Conversely, any direct revelations or messages from God were integrated into daily living and expected personal and national response.

Right from the time of the founding of the Israelite nation, the Scriptures make it clear that everyone was expected to know God's word, and also to be involved in the process of teaching it to others. In this connection, the passage in Deuteronomy 6:1–9 is very instructive. The Israelite people were to obey God and keep his commandments with all their heart, soul, and strength to show that they loved him. They were to teach these laws to their children, but of course, in order to be able to teach their children, they had to know the laws themselves. This was not to be done by referring to a book, but these laws had to be in their hearts (v. 6); in other words, memorized. Then the verses point out how the laws of God were expected to be an integral part of all their daily living.

> Impress them on your children. Talk about them when you sit at home and when you walk along the road, when you lie down and when you get up. Tie them as symbols on your hands and bind them on your foreheads. Write them on the doorframes of your houses and on your gates. (vv. 7–9)

As we look through the Old Testament we see many examples of God's word being presented in ways that were appropriate for these oral communicators to receive.

Genealogies were recorded to remind Israel of the people who were important in their history. Significant events and teachings were prepared as songs. Moses and Miriam prepared songs for all of Israel to sing after their deliverance from slavery in Egypt (Ex 15:1–21). Deborah and Barak did the same after a victory in battle (Judg 5). The Psalms are an extensive theological hymnbook. The prophets, such as Isaiah, Jeremiah, Daniel, and Jonah, prepared their messages in the form of poems, songs, stories, acted dramas, and parables. Books such as Job, Proverbs, Song of Solomon, and Ecclesiastes are other examples of unique theological literature prepared with an oral community in mind. But what stands out as we consider these Scriptures is that this is *the word of God structured for remembrance*!

The above helps us to understand a little about the audiences that received "the Divine Word in human words." Now we will consider in more detail just how those human words were presented.

THE NATURE OF OLD TESTAMENT LITERATURE

Old Testament literature contains a remarkable variety of forms, and this reflects the richness of the people's culture (Linton 1979, 132).

Poetry

Many people from Western societies seem to find it unusual that there is so much poetry in the Bible. But this is largely due to the Western worldview and the fact that most people give poetry a low priority rating when they consider important forms of communication. However, the Old Testament is thoroughly permeated with it, and this tells us again that the audiences of that time were oral communicators, and poetry was a high priority with them. In fact it was probably one of the most ancient as well as one of the most honoured forms of communication used in Israel's history.

> The reason for the relative antiquity of verse is very simple: poetry was then regularly sung or chanted to the accompaniment of stringed instruments such as the harp and the lyre, especially various forms

of the lyre, which were known in both Egypt and Babylonia before the middle of the third millennium. Since the lyre appears in rock carvings in central Arabia at an even earlier date, it must have been known in Mesopotamia from Chalcolithic, if not Neolithic, times. Illustrations of the priority of verse are innumerable. (Albright 1965, 2)

Biblical poetry has many features, including the following (see Linton 1979, 132–35):

- *Synonymous parallelism*, in which the concept expressed in the first line is repeated in the second with different words or concepts. For example, "The LORD watches over you— / the LORD is your shade at your right hand" (Ps 121:5).
- *Antithetical parallelism*, in which the concept expressed in the first line is reinforced in the second by the introduction of an opposite concept. For example, "Fear of man will prove to be a snare, / but whoever trusts in the LORD is kept safe" (Prov 29:25).
- *Synthetic parallelism*, in which the second member complements or adds to the first. For example, "You will be secure, because there is hope; / you will look about you and take your rest in safety" (Job 11:18).
- *Climactic parallelism*, in which the second member and possibly those following reinforce the theme by comparisons with what was affirmed first. For example, "There are six things the LORD hates, / seven that are detestable to Him" (Prov 6:16).

The significance of these poetic features, and of the poetry itself, is that as the people sang or chanted, or said these things many times over, they were remembered, and in turn passed on to the next generation.

In addition to their function in enhancing literary beauty, parallelism and repetition are often used as mnemonic devices. In an age when writing was hard to achieve and hard to preserve, entire cultural heritages, including wisdom literature, were preserved orally, including laws, genealogies, and history, from generation to generation, with astonishing faithfulness. (Linton 1979, 134–35)

Narrative

This occupies a central place in the Bible and ranges from long historical passages to vivid storytelling, such as the story of Joseph in Genesis 37–50, and through to short stories and parables. In the narratives of the Bible we have supreme examples of how a story should be told.

> The LORD sent Nathan to David. When he came to him, he said, "There were two men in a certain town, one rich and the other poor. The rich man had a very large number of sheep and cattle, but the poor man had nothing except one little ewe lamb he had bought. He raised it, and it grew up with him and his children. It shared his food, drank from his cup and even slept in his arms. It was like a daughter to him.
>
> "Now a traveller came to the rich man, but the rich man refrained from taking one of his own sheep or cattle to prepare a meal for the traveler who had come to him. Instead, he took the ewe lamb that belonged to the poor man and prepared it for the one who had come to him."
>
> David burned with anger against the man and said to Nathan, "As surely as the LORD lives, the man who did this must die! He must pay for that lamb four times over, because he did such a thing and had no pity."
>
> Then Nathan said to David, "You are the man!" (2 Sam 12:1–7)

Stories like this, as well as other narrative sections, were composed with great oral skills of conciseness, vividness, and perception of human nature and needs. They were not difficult to memorize and became a part of the living, oral heritage of the Israelite people.

Drama

Although the Bible stories are not actually scripted in modern dramatic format, the whole Bible is itself a drama, and each story lends itself very readily to dramatization. The stories are true to life and can be adapted and presented to audiences of almost any society in the world. Books such as Ruth, Esther, Job, and Jonah are all real-life dramas, and it is quite probable that they were presented as such to the Israelite audiences of those days. The following extract from Jonah almost reads as if it were scripted for a play.

> Then the sailors said to each other, "Come, let us cast lots to find out who is responsible for this calamity." So they cast lots and the lot fell on Jonah. So they asked him, "Tell us, who is responsible for making all this trouble for us? What kind of work do you do? Where do you come from? What is your country? From what people are you?"

> He answered, "I am a Hebrew and I worship the LORD, the God of heaven, who made the sea and the dry land."

> This terrified them and they asked, "What have you done?" (They knew he was running away from the LORD, because he had already told them so.)

> The sea was getting rougher and rougher. So they asked him, "What should we do to you to make the sea calm down for us?"

> "Pick me up and throw me into the sea," he replied, "and it will become calm. I know that it is my fault that this great storm has come upon you." (Jonah 1:7–12)

Drama is a very dynamic form of communication, and through these dramas the Israelite people were able to identify closely with the people involved and so apply God's message directly to their own lives. Today there is great potential for using these dramas in just the same way in many oral cultures around the world.

SOME EXAMPLES OF OLD TESTAMENT SCRIPTURE PRESENTATIONS

We will now consider, in a little more detail, some specific examples of Old Testament Scripture presentations to see just how the various literary forms were used to communicate effectively to the Israelite audience. These literary forms also provided oral structures that would enable those oral communicators to remember the messages and so preserve them as part of their cultural literary heritage.

Genesis

The following are just two samples of literary forms used in Genesis. They are quite distinctive forms of oral communication, but Western, literacy-oriented people would probably ignore them or not even recognise their presence.

Genealogies

Genesis, the book of beginnings, divides clearly into two sections on the basis of content. Chapters 1–11 deal with the primeval history, and chapters 12–50 tell us of the patriarchal history. But as we look at the literary structure we find that the book divides into ten sections, each section being identified by a "*toledoth* [descendants] formula"—"And these are (this is) the descendants (or story) of . . ." (Gen 2:4; 5:1; 6:9; 10:1; 11:10,27; 25:12,19; 36:1,9; 37:2)—in other words, a *genealogy* (see LaSor, Hubbard, and Bush 1982, 68).

For modern Westerners, genealogies may seem terribly uninteresting, but for the Israelites of that time, and for people of many other similar societies, the genealogies are really exciting, because for them they are the key to their own personal and national identity. So not only does this arrangement arouse interest, it also provides a memory device that will enable the hearers to learn the whole content of the book.

We might think that learning all the genealogies of Genesis would be a very formidable task, but for the Melanesians I know, apart from the difficulty of pronouncing some of the names, this would be a rather straightforward assignment and one they would enjoy immensely. So it would have been for the Israelites of that time.

Creative Commands

It is of great interest to look carefully at the account of creation in Genesis chapter 1. LaSor, Hubbard, and Bush have described it as follows:

> Chapter 1, for example, consists of a highly structured series of succinct, almost formulaic, sentences whose components can easily be separated out and outlined. Each creative command consists of:

- an introductory word of announcement,
    "God said . . ." (1:3,6,9,11,14,20,24,26).
- a creative word of command,
    "let there be . . ." (1:3,6,9,11,14f.,20,24,25).
- a summary word of accomplishment,
    "God made . . .," "the earth brought forth . . ." (1:4,7,12,16–18,21,25,27).
- a descriptive word of naming or blessing,
    "God called . . .," "God blessed . . ." (1:5,8,10,22,28–30).
- an evaluative word of approval,
    "God saw that it was good" (1:4,10,12,18,21,25,31).
- a concluding word of temporal framework,
    "It was evening and it was morning, day . . ."
    (1:5,8,13,19,23,31) . . .

> The whole chapter is not really a "narrative" or story, but a carefully constructed report of a series of commands. (Ibid., 70)

Again, this is a literary device that helps people to remember the content and also to be able to teach it to others.

Jeremiah

The book of Jeremiah is possibly the best example to choose as being representative of the way the prophets used various literary forms. It contains a wide variety of these forms that demonstrate the breadth of Jeremiah's communicational approach to the Israelite people. "Like his fellow prophets, Jeremiah used literary patterns familiar to his hearers, but in fresh and striking combinations that gave his oracles a vitality, a vividness, and an urgency unsurpassed in the Bible" (LaSor, Hubbard, and Bush 1982, 419).

Prose and poetry are skilfully interwoven throughout the book, but it is not difficult to identify the following forms.

Prose
There are a number of forms of prose, with the following being the most prominent.

Prose oracles. These are usually judgement speeches, indictments of sins, and threats of judgement. Often the oracle begins with divine instructions as to where, when, and to whom the message is to be given. For example:

> This is the word that came to Jeremiah from the LORD: "Stand at the gate of the LORD's house and there proclaim this message:
> 'Hear the word of the LORD, all you people of Judah who come through these gates to worship the LORD. This is what the LORD Almighty, the God of Israel, says: Reform your ways and your actions, and I will let you live in this place.'" (Jer 7:1–3)

Salvation speeches. One example of this is Jeremiah 31:31–34, which is the prophecy of the "new covenant." This is a section of prose in the midst of poetry: "'Behold, the days are coming,' says the LORD, 'when I will make a new covenant with the house of Israel and the house of Judah. . . . I will put my law within them, and I will write it upon their hearts. . . .'" (RSV).

Symbolic acts. In Jeremiah 13:1–11 Jeremiah was given a series of instructions about a linen belt, to act out over a period of time, which illustrated God's forthcoming judgement on Judah. Jeremiah had to buy the linen belt, wear it for a time, and then go and bury it in a place that symbolised the corrupting influence of foreign nations and gods. A long time afterwards he had to go and dig it up and show that it was now ruined and useless—a graphic demonstration of what was happening to the nation of Israel.

Other symbolic acts are described in Jeremiah 16:1–18; 19:1–15; 27:1–15. These were powerful dramas, not simply for people's entertainment, but rather as vivid warnings of imminent personal and national judgement. These symbolic acts could probably be better classified as oral events than as literary forms. The actual oral portrayal of these events was far more important and significant to the people than the write-up of them after it was all over.

Autobiographical and biographical narratives. These form a large part of this book and include the account of the prophet's call, told in the first person (Jer 1:4–19), and the description of Jehoiakim's burning of Baruch's scroll (Jer 36:1–32), both of which are vivid and graphic accounts.

> The word of the LORD came to me, saying,
>
> "Before I formed you in the womb I knew you,
>   before you were born I set you apart;
>   I appointed you as a prophet to the nations."

"Alas, Sovereign LORD," I said, "I do not know how to speak; I am too young."

But the LORD said to me, "Do not say, 'I am too young.' You must go to everyone I send you to and say whatever I command you. Do not be afraid of them, for I am with you and will rescue you," declares the LORD.

Then the LORD reached out his hand and touched my mouth and said to me, "I have put my words in your mouth. See, today I appoint you over nations and kingdoms to uproot and tear down, to destroy and overthrow, to build and to plant." (1:4–10)

These accounts read like dramas, but they also reveal the intense personal and emotional relationship of the prophet with God and with his message.

Historical narratives. These give details of Judah's history, such as in Jeremiah 38:28–39:18, which tells of the fall of Jerusalem:

This is how Jerusalem was taken:

In the ninth year of Zedekiah king of Judah, in the tenth month, Nebuchadnezzar king of Babylon marched against Jerusalem with his whole army and laid siege to it. And on the ninth day of the fourth month of Zedekiah's eleventh year, the city wall was broken through. Then all the officials of the king of Babylon came and took seats in the Middle Gate: Nergal-Sharezer of Samgar, Nebo-Sarsekim a chief officer, Nergal-Sharezer a high official and all the other officials of the king of Babylon. When Zedekiah king of Judah and all the soldiers saw them, they fled; they left the city at night by way of the king's garden, through the gate between the two walls, and headed toward the Arabah.

But the Babylonian army pursued them and overtook Zedekiah in the plains of Jericho. They captured him and took him to Nebuchadnezzar king of Babylon at Riblah in the land of Hamath, where he pronounced sentence on him. There at Riblah the king of Babylon slaughtered the sons of Zedekiah before his eyes and also killed all the nobles of Judah. Then he put out Zedekiah's eyes and bound him with bronze shackles to take him to Babylon. (38:28–39:7)

These narratives provide important historical details, but they also communicate the mood, tensions, and "atmosphere" of the particular events, an important characteristic of effective oral communication technique.

Poetry

Poetry is a major part of Jeremiah's presentation, and these are not uniform but include a wide variety of forms. We will just mention a couple of these.

Judgement speeches. These could be in the form of an admonition—

> Let everyone beware of his neighbour,
>   and put no trust in any brother;
> for every brother is a supplanter,
>   and every neighbour goes about as a slanderer. (Jer 9:4 RSV)

—or in the form of a rhetorical question:

> Shall I not punish them for these things? says the LORD;
>   and shall I not avenge myself
>   on a nation such as this? (Jer 9:9 RSV)

Salvation speeches in poetry. These give promise of hope and deliverance for Judah and descriptions of restoration.

> Thus says the LORD:
> Behold, I will restore the fortunes of the tents of Jacob,
>   and have compassion on his dwellings;
> the city shall be rebuilt upon its mound,
>   and the palace shall stand where it used to be. (Jer 30:18 RSV)

There are many other literary techniques used throughout Jeremiah. But these suffice to illustrate that Jeremiah spoke to his own generation in ways that were culturally relevant and compelling. Not only that, but his messages were remembered for many generations and later recorded in written form for posterity.

THE WRITINGS

The order for this collection of books in the present Hebrew Bible is as follows: Psalms, Job, Proverbs, Ruth, the Song of Solomon, Ecclesiastes, Lamentations, Esther, Daniel, Ezra, Nehemiah, and 1 and 2 Chronicles. A large portion of the Writings is poetic, and much of it was used by the Israelites in public worship. These materials were particularly relevant to the Israelite community, because they reflected the responses of God's people to his working in their lives. Because they were prepared in oral communicational forms, they could be sung or chanted or recited over and over again and applied by the people to their own personal lives.

> Bless the LORD, O my soul;
> and all that is within me, bless his holy name!
> Bless the LORD, O my soul,
> and forget not all his benefits. (Ps 103:1,2 RSV)

> In the LORD's hand the king's heart is a stream of water
> that he channels toward all who please him.
> A person may think their own ways are right,
> but the LORD weighs the heart. (Prov 21:1,2)

> Like an apple tree among the trees of the forest
> is my beloved among the young men.
> I delight to sit in his shade,
> and his fruit is sweet to my taste.
> Let him lead me to the banquet hall,
> and let his banner over me be love. (Song 2:3,4)

The above classic statements from the Psalms, Proverbs, and Song of Solomon are typical of the literary riches contained in the Writings. But they are literary riches that were not there simply to be admired. They were used by the Israelite people in their individual and corporate worship of God; in their fellowship together as a community of God's people; and in the teaching of their religious beliefs and experiences of God, from one generation to the next.

The Psalms, the wisdom literature, the Chronicler's history, the songs of love and lamentation, the visions of comfort give startling expression to the depths of faith which God expects of his people. The impact of law, prophecy, and history on succeeding generations would have been less powerful had God not also inspired and preserved the emotions, the instructions, even the frustrations of the Writings . . . .

They are an essential part of "all Scripture . . . inspired by God and . . . useful for teaching, for reproof, for correction, and for training in righteousness" (2 Tim 3:16). (LaSor, Hubbard, and Bush 1982, 509)

CONCLUSION

It is fascinating to consider, even briefly, the amazing literature contained in the Old Testament and to see how wonderfully the Holy Spirit superintended the presentation of God's word through human vessels, such as the patriarchs, Moses, the prophets, and people like David and Solomon. In this way the message came to people in forms that were not only vivid and dynamic but that were easily understood and learned.

It is important to remember also that Jesus used many of the same communication forms and skills that are portrayed in the Old Testament. In fact it could be said that he brought them to a pinnacle. Jesus took up the same communication techniques that had been used by the Israelites for many centuries and gave them that quality of divine brilliance that set him apart as the greatest teacher of all time.

This is of considerable significance to us when we realise that more than two-thirds of the present world population are oral communicators, just as the early Israelites were. The literary genius and communication techniques that we have carefully considered in the Old Testament and in the ministry of Jesus are not simply for our admiration and contemplation, but can have very practical significance in bringing God's word to people around the world today. We need to keep these scriptural examples in mind as we consider in more detail the principles that are involved in communicating the Christian message effectively to the people around the world who are members of our contemporary oral societies.

5

PRINCIPLES INVOLVED IN COMMUNICATING TO ORAL SOCIETIES

When we realize that the oral communicators of the world represent a vast array of cultural, religious, economic, social, and political contexts, it may seem presumptuous to talk about specific principles of communication that would apply to them. However, it is important for us to understand that there are basic principles that apply to all types of communication, whether those involved are oral communicators or not. Using these principles as a foundation, we can establish a pattern of communication that relates specifically to oral societies and should be effective. As we establish this pattern, we will find that it reinforces one of the main themes of this book: that the communication techniques that are part of an oral people's culture are the most appropriate to use in the communication of Christian truths to them. These are the same principles of effective communication that Jesus used amongst the oral community of first-century Israel.

MODELS OF COMMUNICATION

The following models are basic to our understanding of the principles of communication.

The S-M-R Process of Communication

The figure below was adapted from Hesselgrave (1978) and Dye (1985, 49) (see also M. Kraft 1978, 77–82). It portrays the basic S-M-R process of communication. Someone (called Source, or S) wants to communicate a meaning (Source Meaning) to one or more people (Receptor, or R). In order to do this he needs to formulate a message (M), and then communicate this message to the Receptor.

As we have already seen, this message can be presented in an incredible variety of ways, and must also take into account many additional messages that are also being communicated at the same time. These include things such as body language, musical accompaniment, the environmental context, the rank or status of the Source, and the rank or status of the Receptor. The Receptor interprets the message and then works out what he believes to be the true meaning of that message (Receptor Meaning). R thinks that this meaning is exactly the same as intended by the Source. Unless S detects something unusual in R's response, he will assume the same thing; that is, that R has worked out the correct meaning of the message. But the true situation usually reveals something different and more complex.

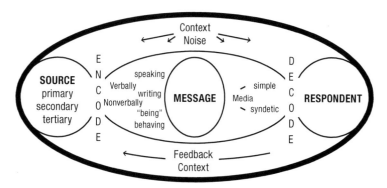

Fig. 3. The S-M-R Process of communication
(Hesselgrave 1978, 51; Dye 1985, 49)

Engel's Model of Interpersonal Communication

James Engel describes a similar model, which indicates some of the activities occurring between the Source (Communicator) and the Receptor (Receiver).

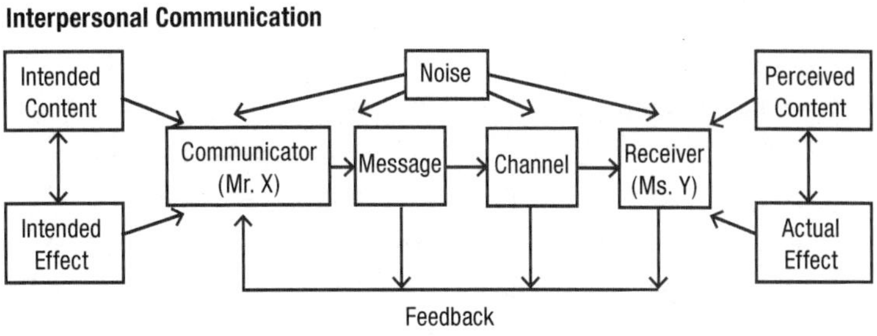

Interpersonal Communication

Fig. 4. Engel's model of interpersonal communication
(Engel 1979, 39)

This model is actually made up from many ideas and models used by a great number of communicators to describe the communication process (Engel 1979, 39). Engel's model includes the important component of feedback. This varies considerably according to the communicational context. In an oral community, for instance, participation by the whole group is usual, so the feedback factor is strong, and this helps to achieve a close parallel between source and receptor meaning.

In Western societies, however, communication is often by means of a presentation where just one person speaks and everyone else listens. In that situation feedback is weak. S assumes R has understood the message correctly, but this is often far from reality. In many cases R will not understand the message correctly, and because there is little opportunity for interaction with S, this incorrect meaning will be retained by R and possibly confirmed by similar messages received later on. This problem is compounded when someone from a Western culture attempts to communicate with people from a different culture who are oral communicators. If only Western ways of communication are used, with little opportunity for interaction between S and R, then the result will probably be a high rate of misunderstanding.

Smalley (1978) and Nida (1954, 1960) are just two of the many researchers who give extensive examples of this kind of miscommunication, such as the following:

> The Shipibos of Peru have an abundance of "How it came to be" stories, and they are constantly on the lookout for any further "mythological" explanations of the world around them. Accordingly,

when they heard the story of the Gerasene demoniacs [*sic*] (Mark 5:1–13) and how the evil spirits were sent off into the swine who forthwith dashed down a cliff into the waters of the lake, they immediately decided that they had an explanation of the origin of dolphins, which they called customarily in their own language "water demons." The whole point of the Biblical story was lost, as far as the Shipibos were concerned, for they were more interested in the presumed origin of dolphins than in what happened to the demoniacs [*sic*]. (Nida 1960, 87)

The Process of Interpretation

Figure 5 helps us to understand what happens in the communication process. The message is interpreted by R through a complex screening process, which is determined by his own cultural environment and worldview. R regards his interpretation of the message as being the true meaning of the message. In describing this process Condon refers to three things that happen:

1. Much of the information received by R is ignored. (This could be for many reasons—meaningless, unimportant, irrelevant, foreign.)

2. R focuses on a limited amount of the information received.

3. R combines or rearranges some of the information received so that it fits into a pattern that is recognised and meaningful to R. (Condon 1975, 20; see also Shaw 1988, 28–35)

The receptor sometimes perceives a meaning quite different from that intended by the source, and the further apart the backgrounds of S and R are culturally, the more likely it is that there will be misunderstanding and wrong interpretation. Charles Kraft summarizes the process this way:

The communicator has certain meanings in his mind that he encodes in cultural symbols (primarily linguistic symbols) and transmits in the form of a message to one or more receptors. The receptors, for their part, decode the message in their heads and thereby derive the meanings on the basis of which they act. (1978, 359)

As indicated above, in Engel's model, if there is the opportunity for feedback and dialogue during the communication process, there is a greater chance of the source meaning and receptor meaning coming to a closer approximation of each other.

The communicator needs to realize that even though the receptor has endeavoured with the utmost sincerity to interpret the source's message correctly, he may not do so, and what is probably more important, he will not even be aware that he has misinterpreted anything.

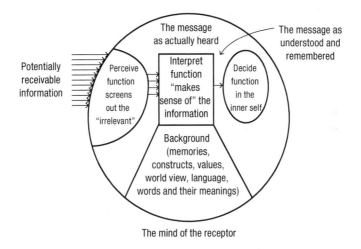

Fig. 5. Details of the interpretation process (Dye 1985)

An important feature of . . . misunderstandings is that the receptor is totally unaware of them. The normal assumption for every person is that the real world is exactly as he perceives it to be; otherwise he would change his perception. The messages he perceives are part of that real world; he also takes it for granted that he is perceiving them correctly. (Dye 1985, 11)

The problems associated with achieving accurate communication are intensified if that communication is cross-cultural. It is further complicated if the Source is endeavouring to introduce new ideas that call for major changes on the part of the receptor. Where the Christian message is concerned, the source would need to be aware that many receptors are already prejudiced against perceiving that anything good or truthful can be associated with that message. This would be the case where the religious context is predominantly

Muslim, Hindu, Buddhist, or Shinto, and would also apply to many of the tribal animistic settings.

PRINCIPLES OF COMMUNICATION

The above models help us to appreciate the complexity of the communication process, and just how difficult the task can be to achieve accurate, effective communication in certain contexts. It also highlights the need for us to establish sound principles as the basis for any communication strategy we may prepare for presenting the Christian message to oral people.

Effective Communication Is Receptor-oriented

Some people who are serious about communicating effectively to other people will make sure they know their subject matter thoroughly, and may also go to considerable lengths to make their presentation a dynamic one, with perhaps visual and multimedia aids. But that is what we could call communicator-oriented communication. The communicator feels confident and comfortable about his knowledge of the subject matter, and its presentation, and also probably feels that his audience does too. However, if we are really concerned that the people to whom we are communicating have a clear understanding of our message, then our whole approach needs to be different, and our focus needs to be on the receptors and what their total perception of the message will be. Charles Kraft is one who strongly emphasises this principle:

> It is the receptor who will make the final judgments concerning what has been communicated. Accuracy and correctness, then, will have to be evaluated at the receptor's end of the communication process even more than at the communicator's. The cultural forms that are employed by the communicator to convey the message, then, will have to be chosen carefully on the basis of the communicator's best understanding of what their impact on the receptor will be. (1979a, 148–49)

> A receptor oriented communicator . . . is careful to bend every effort to meet his receptors where they are. He will choose topics that relate directly to the felt needs of the receptors, he will choose methods of presentation that are appealing to them, he will use language that is maximally intelligible to them. (1983, 6–7)

When we consider this principle in relation to people in oral communities, then all of the characteristics and features of these communities as outlined previously must be brought to bear on the strategy that is adopted when we want to communicate effectively with them. This leads us to consider some principles that flow from the receptor-oriented principle.

The Total Cultural Context of Receptors Must Be Understood

When we talk about total cultural context, we are thinking of the worldview of the people, their linguistic forms, their social structures, and especially all the communicational forms and systems that are part of that cultural context.

In defining culture Nida quotes Robert Redfield:

> The culture of a people is then its total equipment of ideas and institutions and conventionalized activities. The "world view" of a people . . . is the way people characteristically look outward upon the universe. (1954, 85)

Nida then goes on to say, "All these elements in the culture of a people are intimately related to the problems of communication" (1960, 36). If this is so, then a Christian communicator needs to take more than a superficial interest in the culture of the people among whom they are working. If even a small part of a people's culture is misunderstood, or not known at all, there is a good chance that effective communication will be hindered or spoiled. Nida gives an illustration of missionaries working among Native Americans who translated the term "baptism" by the phrase "to brand with water," but to the Native Americans this term carried the idea of ownership, and they were not positive towards that at all! There was, however, a term for "initiation" that could have been used in the context of baptism and would have been much more acceptable to the people.

Nida's emphasis is that communicators need to do thorough research and work with much patience and humility in order to discover the effective means of communication that are there, through the people's own culture. "All too often people have attributed rejection of the Christian message to human perversity or Satanic influence, when in many cases it was due to sheer irrelevancy of the communication" (ibid., 184).

Religion is a very significant part of the total cultural context when we are thinking of communicating the Christian message to people. Nida was prepared to take this very sensitive matter and open it up to sound anthropological and communicational principles. In this way Christians have been able to discover many important things about the religious beliefs of other peoples, and effective ways of communicating the Christian message to them.

> Religion involves an almost incredible variety of activities: bloody sacrifices, mumbled curses, painful ordeals, frightening séances, ecstatic tongues, drunken orgies, fantastic visions, and pomp and ceremony. How to find in all these activities some unifying principle or means of meaningful classification is not easy, especially when the motives of many religious activities are so different, or even contradictory.... Nevertheless, despite the utterly different outward forms and the diametrically opposed motives which prompt religious actions, one basic characteristic runs through all these activities: namely, communication to and from the supernatural. In order to understand how closely communication is linked with religion—how, in fact, it is in large measure the very essence of religious practice—religious activities must be investigated in a wide range of cultural expression. (Ibid., 9–10)

In oral cultures, many of the group and community activities, such as rituals and processions, divination procedures and healing sessions, are connected with religion. The stories, songs, and poems, the dances and dramas, are all related to communication with the supernatural. So it is clear that if we are going to have something relevant to say to these communities about communication to and from God, then it needs to be done orally.

One of the striking messages of the Gospels is that this is exactly what Jesus did with the Israelite people of his time. He was born and raised among them as one of their own people. He understood their cultural context perfectly. And he used their own oral communication system of stories, poetry, songs, parables, and dialogue with dynamic impact. This is an example of effective communication that we cannot ignore.

The *medium* used to send a message is also a very significant part of the cultural context of any group. Each medium itself carries an impact, or "message" (see McLuhan 1966). This is quite distinct from the content of the material being presented by that medium. In most cases people are unaware of how deeply they are affected by the impact of the medium, and tend to focus more on what is being presented by it. In oral communities especially, where so much of the communication media is aural and involves participation by live performers and an audience, the receptors will respond to the medium used in each case, and they will quickly sense whether or not it is the right sort of medium to use in that situation. For Western Christian communicators, this is most important, as we need to consider not only the possibility of the negative impact of Western communication forms on the people to whom we are seeking to minister, but also the positive impact of cultural communication forms that may not have been tried.

The Cognitive Processes of Receptors Must Be Understood

Hesselgrave, in his book *Communicating Christ Cross-culturally*, has a very important section on cognitive processes, in which he points out that different people groups think differently. In this he is not referring to small differences in people's understanding, but quite major differences in their thinking processes. If we are concerned about effective communication, then it is obvious that we need to understand the thinking processes of our receptors. Hesselgrave describes three major approaches to the way people think about reality:

1. The Conceptual: . . . corresponds with the theoretical or logical reasoning. . . . [P]eople analyze reality systematically by means of lineal logic and progression. Abstract terminology and ideas are prominent. This approach to reality is identified with the west.
2. The Intuitional or Psychical: . . . emphasises intuition and the knowledge that emanates from inner experience and vision. This approach to reality is identified with Hindu and Buddhist philosophy.
3. Concrete Relational Thinking: . . . life and reality are seen pictorially in terms of the active emotional relationships present in a concrete situation. This approach to reality is identified with tribal and oriental people. (1978, 207–8)

Broadly speaking, we could say that oral communicators are either category 2 or 3, or a combination of these two, and literacy-oriented communicators are category 1.

The Development of Conceptual Thinking

It would be helpful at this point to describe in a little more detail what conceptual thinking is, and also how it came about. This may help those of us who are in that category to understand more clearly why people with other thinking processes have such difficulty in communicating with us.

Written language has been around for a long time. The Sumerians developed a script in Mesopotamia around 3500 BC. Their script used a symbol to represent a thing. The Semitic peoples produced a phonetic alphabet about 1500 BC. Their script used a symbol to represent a sound. This was quite a radical change in the mental processing of information supplied by the script. Instead of instant recognition of a symbol and its meaning, symbols had to be arranged in correct sequence in order that they could be recognised by sound as a word and the appropriate meaning given to it. In a script of this nature the words also have to be arranged in correct grammatical sequence so that the right meaning is understood.

Arabic and Hebrew are languages developed in the Middle East that have blended in well with the oral cultures of those people. They did not have full vowels, so they could not be written very precisely and were dependent on the context for a full understanding of the meaning. The Greek alphabet, which was introduced about 700 BC, was much more complete than Arabic and Hebrew, and allowed the users to be much freer of the context. So it was this type of script that ushered in abstract and analytical thought, and its use enabled new thought patterns to develop, which eventually resulted in Greek philosophy. By about 400 BC, at the time of Plato, there was a conscious differentiating of the oral and literate worlds, so much so that Plato wanted to exclude poets from his imagined republic. He rejected the oral-oriented thinking perpetuated by poets like Homer and preferred the analytical abstract reasoning of philosophy and the logical processing of thought itself, which was made possible by the alphabet being internalized in the Greek mind. However, up until the Renaissance and the advent of the alphabetic movable-type printing press, only a small minority of people who became fully literate, and although they had a significant influence on their society, the great majority of people remained oral communicators.

With the introduction of mass printing about AD 1500, and the availability of reasonably priced literature for a wide stratum of society, a complete change came upon Western society as it was permeated by the influence of the printed phonetic alphabet. The widespread use of literature demanded that people develop a greater ability to use a systematic, literacy-oriented method to process information in their minds. This information then had to be presented more concisely and precisely in order to be committed to paper. The ultimate result of this was a major worldview shift on the part of the majority of people in Western society. Another result was the great technological gap that developed between the heavily literate West and the oral societies of what we now call "developing countries."

> In the West by the eighteenth century the commitment of sound to space initiated with alphabetic script and intensified by movable alphabetic type had discernibly altered man's feeling for the world in which he lived and for his way of relating to his surroundings. (Ong 1981, 63)

In all of this we can understand that full literacy is a process that requires lengthy preparation in order to achieve clear understanding and considerable energy to use it. There are many advantages gained by its use, but it demands considerable adaptation of a person's thinking processes. To be a proficient reader a person must be able to differentiate clearly between shapes, which is a precise digital type of operation. It is this differentiating function that is the dominant characteristic of literate information processing. People who are truly literate have trained their minds to differentiate whole words by sight rather than sounding them and using resonance to recognise them.

> Sight's ideal is clarity and distinctness for differentiation, measurement and analysis. Sound's ideal is harmony and integration. Sight reveals the outside; the surface conditions. Sound reveals interior conditions; of both things around us and our inner being. (Wiseman 1987b, 2–3)

The above description shows how conceptual thinking developed from literacy, and the availability of printed materials to the masses through the invention of the alphabetic movable-type printing press. But it is almost impossible to assess the consequences that resulted from this basic change in people's thinking processes and the enormous effects on our world, educationally, economically, politically, and spiritually (see Eisenstein 1979; Ong 1982; Schwartz 1972; Wiseman 1987a, 1987b).

The significant thing for us to notice is that because Western society gained educational and economic dominance through the development of conceptual thinking, it has also concluded that this thinking process is superior to others. Without going into lengthy debate on this issue, it would be fair enough to say that each cognitive process has its advantages as well as shortcomings, and that one is not necessarily superior to any of the others. The important thing to know is that they are different, and as communicators, we cannot expect people from any of these categories to be overly enthusiastic about trying to understand or adopt the thinking processes from any of the other categories. This has been a problem with many Christian communicators from Western countries, as they have used conceptual thinking as the basis of their communication strategy and also taught it to their oral-oriented receptors as a superior system to use in communicating the Christian message to others.

Where our focus is on communicating to oral, event-oriented cultures, it is important that we understand that they are nonconceptual in their thinking processes and plan our strategy accordingly. Hesselgrave relates this understanding of the cognitive processes to achieving effective communication with one group of oral communicators, the "concrete relational thinkers."

> It is not just *who* says *what* to *whom*, but *how* the message is channelled to the respondents that determines how the message will be decoded. Language is basic to communication but language does not stand alone. As we have said, words are augmented by pictures, actions, sounds, silence, smells and objects. Words can be spoken or written; pictures can be drawn on canvas or projected on a screen; and actions can be part of sign language for the deaf or part of a stage play. . . .

> Perhaps one of the most challenging areas for missionary exploitation in communicating Christ is to be found in the less sophisticated media which missionaries of the electronic age are apt to overlook— drama, diagrams, drawings and so on. Simple media of this kind are especially important in cultures where concrete-relational thinking predominates and where sophisticated media are difficult for the indigenes themselves to use or fully comprehend. (1978, 391)

In non-Western areas such as Asia and the Middle East, there is a mixture of concrete relational thinking and intuitional thinking. These cultures are full of myths, parables, aphorisms, fables, analogies, similes, metaphors, and tribal lore, as well as a love for ritual and ceremony. There is also a strong element of mysticism, which reveals itself in activities like ancestor veneration, belief in charms, fortune-telling, and sorcery. Depending on location, this mysticism can have a link with the great Eastern religions of Hinduism or Buddhism; or as in many cases where Islam is the state religion, there is an underlying basis of animism.

In settings where the receptors of the Christian message are not conceptual thinkers, it is a poor strategy on our part if we attempt to communicate using a program based on conceptual ideas. In so doing we are asking such receptors to make major adjustments to their own thinking processes if they are going to understand the message clearly. Do we really have that commission or authority, to ask people to make those sorts of fundamental changes? Or should we, as Christian communicators, be the ones to do the adapting and changing? The appropriate thing to do is to plan a program with the receptors' thinking processes in focus, and for us as communicators to make whatever adjustments are necessary.

Again, as we examine carefully the communication techniques of Jesus, we perceive that he used the same thinking processes as his audience; that is, a concrete relational process. His teaching is full of stories, parables, metaphors, and similes based on the people's day-to-day experiences, such as sheep and shepherds (Luke 15:1–7), lamps and oil (Matt 25:1–13), and a wedding and its attendants (Matt 22:1–14). Jesus didn't try to change the thinking processes of his audience; he just made very effective use of what was already there!

The Behavioural Patterns of Receptors Must Be Understood

> Since communication consists not only of a message, but occurs between participants, there are inevitably a number of psychological factors in communication which must be understood if one is to comprehend the true nature of the communicative event. (Nida 1960, 158)

This may appear to be a rather obvious statement, but the fact is that this aspect of communication has received very little attention, especially from Christian communicators. Psychology has been viewed by Christians with even greater suspicion and caution than anthropology. This has not helped us to achieve effective Christian communication, as the statement of Nida above reminds us. Communication is between people, and therefore understanding the behavioural patterns and responses of people is of vital importance. This is especially so when the people communicating are from widely differing cultures and languages.

Jesus understood the behavioural response of his audience only too well, and discerned clearly the genuine from the superficial. The widow who put her mite into the temple offering (Luke 21:1–4) and the people who followed him in the hope of gaining food (John 6:26) are just two examples. History attests the wisdom of Jesus' choice of his disciples as well as his communication techniques. Both of these choices were strongly influenced by his understanding of the behaviour of the people among whom he lived and how he knew they would respond.

Nida discusses such things as "The Psychological Attitudes of the source and the receptor toward the Symbolic System of the Message"; in other words, he asks the question, what behavioural responses are shown by the source and the receptor towards the languages used in the communication process? He also discusses "The Psychological Attitudes between source and receptor," which focuses particularly on the matter of identification by the source with his message and with the receptor (ibid., 158–70). Hesselgrave also points to this as an important factor in cross-cultural communication, and mentions seven aspects of behaviour that need consideration: physical characteristics, body motion, touching behaviour, spatial relationships, temporal relationships, paralanguage, and artefacts and environmental factors (1991, 413–43).

If our receptors are literacy-oriented people and we are endeavouring to communicate to them by means of books and other printed materials, then some of the concerns about behavioural patterns can perhaps be minimized. But if our receptors are oral communicators, then all of the above aspects of behaviour are vital considerations in the whole communications process.

The Decision-making Processes of Receptors Must Be Understood

Many Western Christian communicators go into a cross-cultural situation with preconceived ideas about how the receptors will make decisions about things, and this inevitably affects their whole communication strategy to those people.

In our communication of the Christian message to people, we are asking them to make major decisions about many aspects of their personal and public life. We often assume that receptors will follow an individualistic approach to these decisions, as is typical in literacy-oriented societies. Especially concerning matters of faith and spiritual experience, we believe that people are "captains of their own souls" and will therefore respond to these matters as individuals. Now while we understand that each person is an individual in God's sight, and personally responsible before him for their own spiritual responses to his working in their life, many people, and in particular oral communicators, do not see decision making about these matters to be an individual thing at all. An example from Papua New Guinea is typical of many oral communities around the world. In most Papua New Guinean villages, the various decision making levels are:

1. Matters of no importance which affect no one else—made on personal level.
2. Matters of importance but not affecting the whole village—clan or extended family level.
3. Matters of major importance affecting the whole village—made at level of village.

In any of the meetings (formal or informal) required to make decisions on levels (2) or (3), the pattern is fairly standard. Every man in the group has free expression on the subject while the women listen in (if they are present). Sometimes the women are allowed to voice an opinion they feel very strongly about.

After the topic has been discussed thoroughly, one of the big men, who probably has been a silent listener up to this point, will voice the consensus as a decision which the group then embraces as its decision. Any worthwhile decision is made in this way. (Hovey 1978, 2)

So, if we are looking for meaningful and worthwhile decisions to be made by people in oral communities, then we need to structure our communications strategy in such a way that decisions made by the people about spiritual matters follow the same pattern as decisions normally made in those oral communities. These decisions should be properly consummated and recognised, and then flow on to bring the people to a more advanced stage of Christian growth and maturity.

Meanings Are Not Transmitted, Only Messages

Many communicators operate under the illusion that they are communicating *meaning*, but as we examine the basic principle of communication we can see that this is not the case. The *source* has a *meaning* in his mind. This is then prepared as a *message* and communicated to the *receptor*. It is then up to the *receptor* to construct the *meaning* he perceives from that *message* (see ch. 7 on training nonliterate leaders).

> Meanings lie within people, not in either the external world or the symbols in terms of which we describe that world. Meaning is, therefore, a personal thing, internal to persons rather than part of the world outside. Messages, constructed of symbols, may come from outside a person, but the meanings attached to message symbols are attached or even created within the minds of the persons who receive them. (C. Kraft 1983, 111–13)

Kraft also explains how that meaning is the result of interpretation by the receptor. This interpretation is the subjective interaction of one or more people within a communication situation or event. People make their interpretations and construct their meanings quite independently of each other, but they are usually in harmony with the behaviour and worldview they share with other members of their community (see ibid.).

> Communicators present messages via cultural forms (symbols) that stimulate within the receptors' heads meanings that each receptor shapes into the message that he or she ultimately hears. Meanings are not transmitted, only messages. For "meanings are not in the message, they are in the message-users" (Berlo 1960, 175). The meanings and their organization into received messages come from the interaction between the stimulus of what the communicator says and does and the experience-conditioned understanding facilities of the receptor. The symbols employed function not to contain the meanings but to stimulate meanings within the mind of the receptor

that correspond as closely as possible with those in the mind of the communicator. (C. Kraft 1979a, 148)

This same principle is put forward by Wiseman in his description of a "Resonance" model of communication:

> We are in a continual communication environment, with sounds and sights bombarding us relentlessly. Information is already stored in our brains, some in symbolic forms, but more in the images and patterns in which they were received. (1987a, 37)

> The critical task is to design our package of stimuli so that it resonates with information already stored within an individual and thereby induces the desired learning or behavioural effect. That which we put into the communication has no meaning in itself. The meaning of our communication is what a listener or viewer gets out of the communicator's stimuli. (Schwartz 1972, 25)

> Meaning is evoked when incoming information resonates with resident information. (Wiseman 1987a, 38)

This emphasises to us just how important it is for us to know the people to whom we are communicating. If they are the ones who are creating meaning from the messages we give them, then we certainly need to know everything we can about how and why they are creating that meaning.

Communication Is Most Effective When Communicator and Receptor Participate in the Same Frame(s) of Reference

This principle follows on closely from the previous one, as it underlines the fact that if communicator and receptor are participating in the same frame(s) of reference, or life situation, then there is a strong possibility of there being a close correspondence between the meaning intended by the source and that perceived by the receptor. For the purposes that we have under consideration here, the most effective communication will take place when the source and the receptor are participating in the life situation of the oral society.

The sharing of cultural, subcultural, linguistic, and experiential frames of reference maximizes the possibility that the cultural forms/symbols employed to transmit messages will mean the same thing to both the communicator and receptor. (C. Kraft 1979a, 149–52)

However, the real situation is that people live in many different contexts or life situations, and when people from one life situation attempt to communicate with those from a different life situation, there are often major communication problems. The reason is that all the cultural forms or symbols that people use to communicate derive their meanings from the life situation in which they participate. So if effective communication is going to take place, both the source and the receptor must be able to attach the same or similar meanings to the forms or symbols that are employed. This would normally require them to operate within the same life situation.

When people belong to different cultures or subcultures, the lack of agreement concerning the meanings of linguistic and cultural items severely hampers communication. . . . The frame of reference chosen for the communication can be that of either participant but with a different impact, depending on whose set of categories is employed. If the communicator demands that it be his (or hers), rather than the hearer's frame of reference . . . categories, the approach may be labelled "extractionist" . . . .

If, instead of this extractionist approach, the communicator adopts the receptor's frame of reference . . . we may label the approach "identificational." In this approach communicators become familiar with the conceptual framework of the receptor and attempt to fit their communication to the categories and felt needs of that frame of reference. (Ibid., 149–52)

This principle helps us to understand that it is not only a matter of knowing our receptors but also of being there, experiencing and participating in their lifeworld, which is also known as the "life involvement" or "incarnational" approach.

"Life involvement" . . . is a long term association between communicator and receptors in a variety of life situations, many of which might be quite informal and not highly dependent upon verbalization as the only means of communication. Discipleship and apprenticeship are examples of this kind of communicational method. In discipleship the teacher spends long periods of time with his disciples in a wide variety of life activity. Jesus and his disciples were together twenty-four hours a day for three years. In apprenticeship, an apprentice spends long periods of time with his teacher in a variety of work related activities. (C. Kraft 1983, 46)

Behind the meanings of the Bible and Christian experience that can be translated lie deeper meanings that can be expressed only in greater life involvement between communicators and receptors than translation allows. This life involvement includes linguistic communication but is not, at its most effective, limited to mere verbalization. The verbalization that does occur . . . is most effective when it is most closely related to the personal experience of the participants. (C. Kraft 1979a, 276)

It is only when literacy-oriented communicators take those steps of involvement and participation in the lifeworld of oral communicators that they start to realize the tremendous variety and complexity of communicational possibilities that are there, and what are going to be the appropriate communication forms to use in an effective strategy to bring the Christian message to those people. An important factor involved in participating in the receptor's frame of reference is that the communicator can discover what are known as the "felt needs" of the receptors, individually and as a group.

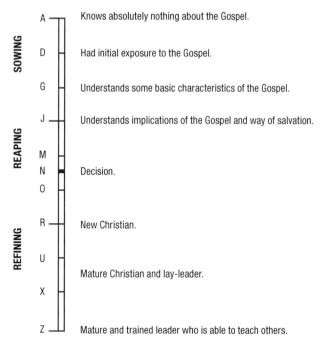

Fig. 6. Model of spiritual segmentation
(Søgaard 1975, 29)

"Felt needs" are what the receptors themselves perceive as their priority needs. In many cases people do not see the spiritual need of salvation and peace with God as a priority need and therefore do not regard the Christian message as relevant or important. However, most would regard spiritual realities as important, and they would participate regularly in religious observances, to deal with felt needs linked to these spiritual realities. "Felt needs" can be very extensive in scope and may include the following:

- *Economic needs:* Poverty and hunger, unemployment, money management.
- *Political needs:* Injustice and oppression from political, social, or religious groups.
- *Health and education needs:* Physical ailments and suffering, hygiene and disease prevention, illiteracy and consequent unemployment or exploitation.
- *Social needs:* Alcohol and drug abuse, marriage and family problems, racial or ethnic conflicts.

- *Spiritual needs:* Fear of spirits, sorcery, and superstition. Bondage to religious systems such as Islam and Hinduism.

Another important purpose for participating in the receptor's life situation is so that the communicator can understand where they are in relation to their awareness of the Christian message. Scales like those produced by Søgaard (1975, 29; 1988b) and Engel (1979, 49, 65) can be helpful guidelines. The communicator is then able to prepare messages at the receptor's point of awareness and hopefully lead her or him on to greater understanding and more positive response to the Christian message.

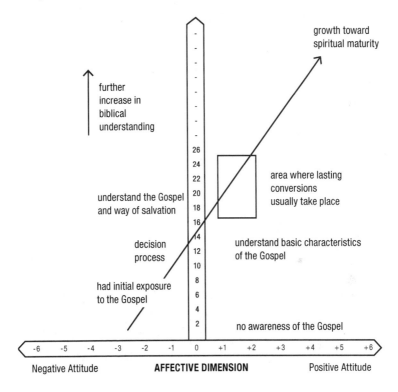

Fig. 7. Strategy and spiritual progress model (Søgaard 1988b)

One of the purposes of Jesus' incarnation among the Israelite people was so that he could participate completely in their life situation. He was able to communicate God's message to them, which was "from above," as a message that came from one of their own people who knew and understood them completely (see Isa 53:1–12; Heb 2:10–18; 4:14–16). Cross-cultural communicators are not able to emulate Jesus' incarnational method, but the principle is there for us to follow. We need to experience and participate in the receptors' life situation if our message is going to have credibility and impact.

As Christian communicators we may say that the most important thing is for people to know Jesus Christ as their Saviour, and then other needs can be addressed. But we must remember that a basic principle of effective communication is that it must be receptor oriented. It is only when we communicate about matters that the receptor sees as important that we will gather interest. When people understand that they are cared for as human beings and not simply as souls to be saved, they are prepared to regard both the communicators and their message as relevant and important.

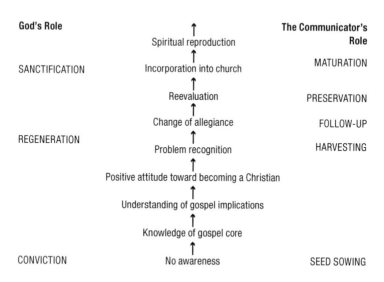

Fig. 8. Decision process model (Engel 1979, 49, 65)

Communication Must Follow Principles of "Dynamic Equivalence"

In such matters as Bible translation, contextualization of the Christian message, theologizing, and church planting, Christians need to employ the principles of "dynamic equivalence." This does not mean that the original context of the Scriptures is to be ignored—far from it—but it does mean that the essential messages of the Scriptures must be "transculturated" or restated in terms of the receptor's cultural setting (see Shaw 1988).

> For today's receptors, Jesus needs to walk their paths, eat in their homes. The receptors need to live and learn, as the original disciples did, in Jesus' presence today. For this they need dynamic witnesses, living and speaking a dynamically equivalent message in terms of the receptors' perceptual grids. (C. Kraft 1979a, 276)

Dynamic equivalence communication to an oral community will mean that the Christian message is brought to that community in such a way that they readily accept it as "their own," and respond to it in the same way that they do to any important message from within their own community. Furthermore, if we take the same communicational form from one cultural context to another we almost invariably change the meaning, and therefore if we wish to transfer the same meaning from one cultural context to another, it is almost essential to change the communicational form.

> Most (probably all) cultural and linguistic forms are interpreted as symbolizing meanings that lie beyond the forms themselves. Any given form, however, is likely to be interpretable in more than one way depending on the context in which it is being used, how it is ordinarily used, how it is suggested it should be used, and/or how the interpreter feels toward it. (C. Kraft 1983, 115–116)

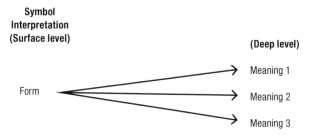

Fig. 9. A given form may have several meanings
(C. Kraft 1983, 117).

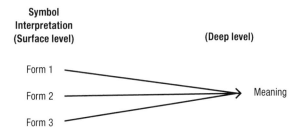

Fig. 10. A given meaning stimulated by more than one form
(C. Kraft 1983, 117)

Both of these principles are of obvious importance in our aim to achieve effective communication. The first principle shows us that whenever we are communicating with people from different backgrounds and life experiences we can expect a variety of interpretations and responses to the same message.

The second principle teaches that we can allow for a number of different presentations of the same message that will basically carry the same meaning. It also means that some groups will prefer a certain communication form because, for cultural or other reasons, they recognise it as their own, and they will probably reject other forms as foreign or inappropriate. This means that in communicating to a particular group we need to use forms that are just as familiar and relevant to them as were the forms used in the original communication context.

> This principle applies whether we are talking about the movement of messages, institutions, music, or other cultural forms from culture/subculture to culture/subculture or from generation to generation. . . .

If the same meaning is to be retained when communicating to another group, the communicator needs to change the forms employed from those appropriate to the first group to those specifically appropriate to the new receiving group. (C. Kraft 1983, 115–19)

When we consider the marked difference between the forms that are appropriate to an oral, event-oriented society and those appropriate to a literacy-oriented society, we can understand that considerable thought and preparation will be needed by literacy-oriented communicators if they are going to produce dynamically equivalent messages for an oral community.

CONCLUSION

Establishing principles for a particular activity can seem to be rather heavy going, especially if we have been anxiously awaiting some action over a long period of time. But the principles are the foundation we lay in order to get the right sort of action. It is important for us to note that Jesus, in all of his communication with the Israelite people, and with his disciples in particular, operated according to effective principles of communication. He was not haphazard or inconsistent, but followed sound principles (see ch. 3).

- He was, above all, receptor oriented.
- He understood their cultural context.
- He understood their cognitive processes.
- He understood their behavioural patterns.
- He understood their decision-making processes (see Mark 1:16–20, the calling of his disciples; Mark 8:34–38, the challenge to discipleship; Mark 10:17–23, Jesus' dialogue with the rich young ruler).
- He participated in the same life situation.
- He ensured that the meaning of his message was understood. (His use of stories and illustrations, his use of dialogue and close interaction with his audience, and especially with his disciples.)
- He ensured that his message and ministry was dynamic (see John 7:46; also "The Galilean Response to Jesus' Ministry," ch. 3).

In the same way as if we were learning to fly an aeroplane, so it is with communication to oral societies; unless we establish the right sort of principles first, the resultant action could be disastrous. In the following chapter we will consider some case studies where the above principles were put into operation and the resultant action was extremely worthwhile.

6

MAKING THE CHRISTIAN MESSAGE
LIVE IN ORAL SOCIETIES

In the previous chapters we have considered a wide range of information about oral communicators. We have talked about their characteristics and communication skills and what sort of communication techniques have been used among them. We have also considered in some detail the communication principles that are necessary if communication with oral people is going to be effective. It could appear that this is a very complex business and that understanding these people and achieving effective communication with them is an impossible task. However, as we shall see, that is far from being the case.

In this chapter we will describe some case studies taken from many different oral communities. These all demonstrate very clearly that the oral communication techniques that are part of the people's own culture are the most appropriate ones to use in the communication of Christian truths within their society. These case studies also show us the remarkable creativity of oral societies. As we examine these case studies, it should be a challenge and an encouragement to those Christians ministering in a cross-cultural context with oral people to see how effective communication can be achieved with the Christian message among those people today.

THE CHRISTIAN MESSAGE LIVING IN ORAL SOCIETIES: CASE STUDIES

Each case study has a heading that indicates its general location and also the type of communication medium that was used. Following each case study is a brief analysis of the strategy used and the communication principles that were employed. The final case study, from the Philippines, is analysed in more detail.

Australia: Drama, Dance, Singing, and Iconographs

We have described briefly some of the oral communication forms of the Warlpiri people of Central Australia (ch. 2). The early perception of Christian missionaries was that these dramas were evil because of their association with pagan rituals and the spirits of the ancestors. Therefore there was strong teaching by the missionaries against using anything from the Aboriginal culture in connection with Christian faith and testimony. The main thrust of mission strategy at that time was to make Aborigines literate in English and attempt to integrate them into Australian society. This strategy was pursued for many years with little success.

Finally, Australian Baptist missionaries working in this area tried something different. Gently but persistently they sought to encourage Aboriginal Christians to use their own culture to express their Christian faith. Progress at the beginning was very slow. There was a lot of resistance to this innovation, by other missionaries and by the Aboriginal people themselves. Also, the actual implementation of this innovation was much more complicated than might at first be expected. The symbols, the songs, the dance movements of their culture—all belonged to different clans. So in order to use any of them, permission had to be granted by the elders of those clans. This required lengthy negotiations. Then, if any new symbols or songs or dance movements were to be used, these had to be accepted by the group.

It was a slow process, but as different things were tried and accepted, and as Christians began to get the feel of using their own culture in this way, they became excited and enthusiastic. A wider and wider range of Aboriginal cultural activities were used, and more and more people became involved. Vernacular Bible translation proved to be incredibly valuable; the vernacular texts were used as the basis for Christian corroborees that tell the stories of the incarnation, trial, death, and resurrection of Jesus.

The enactment of these dramas has to be experienced to really understand its full impact. Organisation and preparation take many hours. Getting all the right people together in the one place at the one time is the first major effort, as traditional Aboriginal cultures have no timetables or agendas in the Western sense. When that is achieved, people are assigned their various parts and the elaborate preparations begin. Numerous attendants assist in putting the body paints, headgear, and other decorations on the participating dancers so that each character is clearly identified. It is a clear example of cooperation and participation by an oral community in a communication event.

An article written about one of these events helps communicate some of the atmosphere and excitement of such an occasion:

> Over 500 people from Darwin, Alice Springs, Yuendumu, Wave Hill, Willowra and Mount Isa assembled at Lajamanu to celebrate Easter and the setting aside of the first Warlpiri missionary to our churches. After a twelve hour bus trip up the Tanami track, the Yuendumu dancers re-enacted the story of the Last Supper and crucifixion of Jesus on Friday night. Saturday evening's celebrations included a new purlapa from Lajamanu which depicted the essence of the Gospel. In creative sign language they portrayed various attempts people try to make to enter God's family. These attempts were rejected by the "church mob" who reminded them that the only way to enter the family was through Jesus.

> After the purlapa the choirs from each community entertained and encouraged weary travellers. It became a late night for those who had been travelling until 3:30 that morning. But tiredness was not to interfere with the proper business of Easter. The resurrection story had to be danced at dawn.

> It is always a time of excitement as the risen Lord comes stamping out victoriously from the grave to show the disciples that He is alive again. The Lord's Supper was celebrated with added meaning as we sat around the stage with the dancers, the excitement of the story

still vividly implanted in our minds. Jesus our Saviour had gloriously risen and was present to share the Celebration. (Ollerenshaw 1986)

The vernacular Scripture texts also became the basis for a series of Bible songs and statements of faith that were put onto audiocassette. These were set to traditional tunes and sung by a group in the traditional manner with a lead singer and response group accompanied by rhythm sticks. As well as the proclamation of gospel stories and messages, this medium began moving into an exciting phase of Christian teaching.

One example is the teaching of Galatians 3:28, "There is neither Jew nor Gentile, neither slave nor free, nor is there male and female, for you are all one in Christ Jesus." To teach this through drama, a large symbol for a person is drawn on the ground (see fig. 11). It would be approximately thirty feet long and thirty feet wide. This represents the person of Christ. The main characters are decorated to indicate exactly who they are—slave, free man, etc.—and they are sitting on the ground outside this figure. The rest of the people sit on the outer perimeter of this "stage," some with boomerangs to beat the rhythm, and they all sing through the phrases of this verse. As they come to the particular characters, such as the Jew and the Gentile, those characters stand, do a brief dance, then move together and sit down inside the symbol of Christ. A few extras are added to the Scripture, such as black and white, rich and poor, young and old. This keeps going until all the people who were outside the symbol are now seated inside. Certainly a vivid way to impress this teaching on anyone!

This medium of oral communication used in their own cultural context has had a marked impact on the whole Aboriginal community in that area. It has gradually affected a wider and wider circle of contacts and hopefully will encourage other groups, with different cultural forms of oral communication, to use those forms for the expression and teaching of their Christian faith.

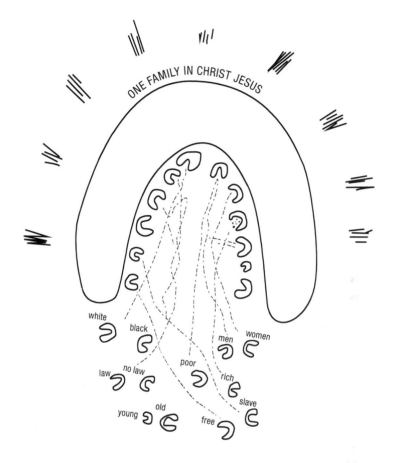

Fig. 11. Iconograph format for teaching Galatians 3:28

Case Study Strategy

The strategy used in this case study and its relationship with the principles of oral communication can be briefly summarized as follows:

- *Cultural context:* Vernacular message. Indigenous art forms: iconographs, songs, drama (corroboree).
- *Frame of reference:* Life involvement of Baptist missionaries with people.
- *Dynamic equivalence:* Scripture presented in indigenous drama form.
- *Group orientation:* Whole community involved in preparation and presentation.

- *Event orientation:* The presentations become important events in the community's life which focus their attention on events and teachings of Scripture.
- *Performance and participation:* Whole community participates in the presentation as well as interaction before and after the events.
- *Biblical models:* As with both New Testament and Old Testament models, the learning and teaching of the scriptural messages does not need any specialised training. Through the iconographs, drama, and singing, it follows the scriptural models of the word of God structured for remembrance.

Colombia: Singing Contests

Bruchko tells the amazing story of a young American missionary, Bruce Olson, who is determined to take God's word to a very fierce tribe, the Motilones, in Colombia. But Bruce wants to do this without disturbing the people's culture. After many hair-raising adventures and much physical suffering, Bruce is eventually accepted by the Motilone people. The climax comes when after about ten years a young man, Bobarishora, who is his "pact-brother," becomes a Christian and decides the time is right to share his faith with his people—but this happens in a way quite unexpected by Bruce:

> Word spread that there was to be another Festival of the Arrows. There was excitement in the home. The festival was the only time all the Motilones gathered together.
>
> Pacts would be formed. Arrows would be exchanged, and the men forming the pact would have a singing contest. They would climb into their hammocks and sing as long as they could, relating legends, stories, and news of recent events. Often their songs would last twelve hours, without interruption for food, water, or rest. . . .
>
> An older chief named Adjibacbayra took a special interest in Bobby [Bobarishora]. . . . On the first day of the festival he challenged Bobby to a song. Bobby was pleased and immediately accepted.
>
> They both climbed into a single hammock twenty feet off the ground and began to swing back and forth. Bobby sang first, and

Adjibacbayra imitated him, following line for line. Other men also had challenged each other to songs and were singing.

Bobby's song was about the way the Motilones had been deceived and had lost God's trail. He told how they had once known God but had been greedy and had followed a false prophet. Then he began to sing about Jesus. As he did so, the other men who were singing stopped. Everyone became quiet in order to listen.

"Jesus Christ was incarnated into man," Bobby sang. "He has walked our trails. He is God, yet we can know Him."

The home was deathly still except for Bobby's wailing song and Adjibacbayra's repetition. People were straining their ears to hear.

Inside me, however, a spiritual battle was raging. I found myself hating the song. It seemed so heathen. The music, chanted in a strange minor key, sounded like witch music. It seemed to degrade the gospel. Yet when I looked at the people around me and up at the chief swinging in his hammock, I could see that they were listening as though their lives depended on it. Bobby was giving them spiritual truth through the song.

Still I wanted to do it *my* way. . . .

When it came to spiritual matters, I thought I had the only way. But my way wasn't necessarily God's way. God was saying, "I too love the Motilone way of life. I made it. And I'm going to tell them about My Son in *My* way."

I relaxed, able at last to find real joy in Bobby's song. It continued for eight hours, ten hours. Attention didn't slacken. It got dark inside the house. Fires were built. Finally, after fourteen hours, they quit singing and climbed wearily down from their hammock.

Adjibacbayra looked at Bobby. "You've communicated a true news item," he said. "I too want to suspend myself in Jesus. I want to pull His blood over my deception."

That night a spiritual revolution swept over the people. No one rejected the news about Jesus. Everyone wanted Him to take them over the horizon. There was tremendous jubilation. . . .

God had spoken. He had spoken in the Motilone language and through the Motilone culture. He had not even had to use me. (Olson 1973, 152–53)

The Motilone society was a typical oral community, reflecting the worldview characteristics discussed in chapter 1. The people were event-oriented. They were group-oriented in participation and response. Communication of something important was done at an appropriate time (the Festival of the Arrows) by means of a culturally relevant form; that is, response singing up in a hammock!

Bruce Olson's response of dislike and discomfort with what was happening was typical of a Western, literacy-oriented person. Even though Olson had identified himself with the people over a number of years, he found it difficult not to respond in this way. However, because he controlled his responses and allowed God to work it out in the culturally appropriate way, he witnessed some very satisfying results.

Case Study Strategy

- *Cultural context:* Message in vernacular. Gospel presentation linked to local cultural values, beliefs, and language ("I too want to suspend myself in Jesus"). Presentation made through indigenous communication form.
- *Decision-making processes:* Gospel presented to the whole group and accepted by the group as a whole.
- *Frame of reference:* Life involvement by expatriate missionary. Developed intimate understanding of cultural values, beliefs, and language, and thus understood people's felt needs.

- *Dynamic equivalence:* Gospel presented through authentic indigenous communication form. This brings about a genuine response: "You have communicated a true news item."
- *Group orientation:* Presentation made at group festival. Group response and decision making.
- *Event orientation:* Presentation made at appropriate group event.
- *Performance and participation:* Presentation made by means of response singing between two men in the midst of an important group event, whereby all could hear and at the appropriate time respond to the message.
- *Biblical models:* The gospel was taught through indigenous singing—the word of God structured for remembrance. Learning and teaching did not require specialised training.

Papua New Guinea: Genealogies

As mentioned in chapter 2, Papua New Guinean people have an extraordinary interest in genealogies. Kevin Hovey, a missionary with the Assemblies of God working in the Sepik District of PNG, was able to combine this interest in genealogies and a culturally adapted visual aid to produce a very effective tool to reach both Christian and non-Christian oral communicators. The visual aid was constructed from a branch of the local sago palm. This has a soft, pithy centre, and into this was placed a line of sticks of various lengths (see fig. 12). Each of the sticks stands for one generation.

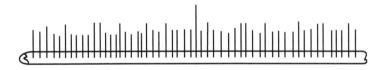

Fig. 12. Kevin Hovey's genealogy stick (1978)

Hovey used this aid to discuss with village groups their own history, church history, and important parts of world history. This then led on to discussion of the life of Jesus on earth and the people and events of Old Testament history, right back to Adam and Eve. In this way Hovey was able to use the people's interest in and understanding of genealogies to communicate to them God's message of salvation in Jesus Christ. The people participated eagerly in the discussions and perceived the message to be relevant and meaningful to them.

During the discussions, which lasted for three or four hours each day, Hovey pointed out the implications of accepting Christian teaching and reminded them that at the conclusion of the meetings they would need to make a decision about what they would do, and that the whole village needed to know about it and agree on it. By the time the meetings concluded, which was usually after about three weeks, the people had made many decisions about the gospel message. Now they made an important decision as a group: to throw all of their charms, fetishes, and other items associated with their previous worship and allegiance into the river. So Hovey's use of a culturally relevant communication form, and his patience and determination to let the people do things their way, was rewarded with a complete turning of these people to Christ.

There are many other details associated with the planning and presentation of the "genealogy stick" stories, but suffice it to say that it was done in a culturally appropriate form. The right people were discussing these things in the right way, and it led to culturally significant decision making (see Hovey 1978). As a result whole villages began to make decisions to become Christians and demonstrated their faith by destroying everything they had that was associated with sorcery and spirit powers. People were open to Christian teaching in a way they had never been before. It was a method that reached the whole spectrum of village life, and for nonliterates especially it was something they could understand and also use to teach others.

Case Study Strategy

- *Cultural context:* Gospel presentation through high-interest cultural value of genealogies. Presentation made in village setting, group discussion with local leaders, gospel related to local issues through genealogy stick.
- *Decision-making process:* Group decision made in cultural manner following presentation.
- *Frame of reference:* Life involvement by expatriate missionary enabled understanding of cultural values and discernment of felt needs that were addressed in presentation.
- *Dynamic equivalence:* Gospel presentation made in terms of high-interest cultural value of genealogies.

- *Group orientation:* Gospel presentation took the form of a group discussion with community leaders having the major input. Whole community involved in decision making.
- *Event orientation:* Genealogy format focused attention on people and events.
- *Performance and participation:* Community leaders participated in genealogy-stick discussions. Whole group participated in follow-up discussions in the homes.
- *Oral communication skills:* Focus was on memory skills and the people's understanding of genealogies.
- *Biblical models:* Learning and teaching did not require special training. Genealogy stick was a memory device enabling the gospel to be structured for remembrance.

Ethiopia: Monologue Reading, Chanting, Singing

Some years ago SIM missionaries in Ethiopia were faced with the prospect of imminent expulsion by the Marxist government of that country. Consequently they planned a strategy of intensive Bible translation and distribution as being the best contribution they could make for the Christian church before they had to leave. This strategy was called the Key Scriptures Translation Project. In brief this meant that, instead of trying to translate the whole New Testament, or whole Bible for any language, key Scriptures would be chosen that would give a balanced and comprehensive presentation of the Christian message.

The Wolayta language was targeted as a priority language for this project because of the high percentage of nonliterates in the group. It was decided that as the translation progressed, it would be recorded on cassette and that cultural communication forms would be used in the presentation. Skilled Christian artists were recruited from among the Wolayta people who could do the musical composition, chanting, singing, and reading that were required. In general the Scriptures were presented with the following format: (a) Monologue reading of verses—about thirty seconds. (b) Cultural chanting of verses—three or four minutes. This was usually done by a lead singer supported by a group. The chanting was structured so that at regular periods a line would be repeated. At this point the group would join in and chant the repeat line with the lead singer. This was also the cue for anyone else who was listening to join in and chant the line along with them. This meant that the whole audience became involved, and therefore the potential for the verses to be accepted and learned was greatly increased. (c) A Scripture song—about one or two minutes. This composition was prepared according to the local musical patterns and usually sung by a soloist. The song was either a key verse from the Scripture passage that had just been heard or else a summary of the teaching of that passage.

Gospel Recordings, Inc. (now Global Recordings Network) was able to provide valuable assistance to SIM in this project. Over a period of two years or so they were able to send into Ethiopia some two thousand hand-wind cassette players. They were distributed throughout the country, and many of them came into the Wolayta area and were used with the cassettes described above. The results of this vernacular Scripture distribution by cassette were extremely encouraging. People responded to their presentation enthusiastically, and they listened to the tapes for hours on end. Before long many of the nonliterate people knew considerable amounts of the Scriptures by heart. The women especially were very excited about the whole concept; they realised that they were no longer cut off from being Bible students and Bible teachers simply because they could not read. They were delighted that in some cases they knew more of the Scriptures than their pastors.

The following story is typical of the way people responded. In the course of making visits in a village, a missionary brought a cassette player and Wolayta tapes into a house where an older man was lying listlessly on his bed. He complained of being ill and hadn't been able to get about for days. The missionary began to play the tape, and the man lifted his head in order to hear better. Soon he was propped up on one elbow, listening intently to every word. Then came a point in the chanting where the whole group responded, and straight away he joined in with them, as his culture compelled him to do. But it wasn't just that he was compelled; he was delighted. Soon he was sitting up straight, all his listlessness had gone, and he was totally absorbed in the presentation. Then he was standing, clapping, chanting, and singing wherever he could, and it was a long time before the missionary could leave and go and visit someone else (see Adams 1980, 5–6).

Case Study Strategy
- *Cultural context:* Message in vernacular. Scripture presentation used indigenous communication forms—chanting, indigenous songs, and group participation.

- *Frame of reference:* Life involvement by expatriate missionaries and indigenous translators ensured Scripture selections and communication forms were culturally relevant and addressed people's felt needs.
- *Dynamic equivalence:* Vernacular Scriptures presented by means of indigenous communication forms.
- *Performance and participation:* Local musicians and singing groups involved in presentation. Communication forms ensured that hearers would participate with appropriate responses.
- *Oral communication skills:* Local composers, musicians, singers, and choirs required for production of Scripture presentation through indigenous communication forms.
- *Biblical models:* Indigenous communication forms and cassette medium meant that everyone could learn and everyone could teach. This also followed the pattern of the word of God structured for remembrance.

South Korea and Thailand: Traditional Drama

At this point it is appropriate to mention some of the reasons why drama is such a significant medium to oral communicators and why Western, literacy-oriented Christians need to be alert to its potential.

Drama is a very ancient part of the fabric of human society. Today it is as influential as ever, perhaps even more so, and for many of us this influence is felt but not noticed. Such is the way of drama; its influence can be subtle but nonetheless significant. Today in Western society there are a number of different perspectives on drama. A small section of society sees drama as art. The majority view it purely as entertainment, and a few Christians see it as a relevant and dynamic medium for communication and expression of their Christian faith.

Some drama is only intended as entertainment, but in most cases drama carries a message. Drama is not only a reflector of society and its values, but a strong influencer. Many recognise the powerful emotional impact of drama and realize how people are able to identify with the characters acting in the drama. So in this way we see drama used to influence people for or against certain values or philosophies. This is seen vividly in the films shown on television and the music videos that promote the lifestyle and values of pop stars and film stars. This is a relatively small group of people, but the influence they have on society through this medium is extremely powerful. As we move into non-Western cultures we find that drama is very often an integral part of the social system. In many cases it is not linked with TV, and the people understand their drama to be personal and relevant to their local situation. Often the whole community is involved in the drama presentation.

However, churches and missions in general are very cautious about the use of drama for evangelism, worship, and other aspects of Christian ministry. In these situations many Christians still equate drama with entertainment and feel therefore that it is not appropriate for Christian witness. For others, there are the problems of previous cultural associations of drama with spirit worship, pagan practices, and immorality. These issues require careful and thorough research in order to be satisfactorily resolved. This is especially so for those who are working amongst nonliterate people. The medium of drama has immense value in communicating Christian concepts and values. The people identify with the characters, and the message speaks to their hearts and is retained in their minds.

It must be kept in mind that the drama has to be related to the people's own cultural expression and be perfectly acceptable to them. And the drama must be done well! To produce good drama in any culture requires commitment and hard work from those involved. Careful research must also be done to ensure that the message communicated carries no wrong or misleading connotations. As Kathleen Nicholls says, "Care must be taken that the form and content together are glorifying to God, and communicate something of his truth to those who participate and those who watch" (1983, 145).

Nicholls tells of a drama group's very effective ministry in South Korea:

> The Bridge Drama Group uses a shadow play called "the Prince of Peace" to portray the life of Christ. On their first tour they showed it to more than 10,000 prisoners and about 4,700 church and school people. This project began when some professional actors were asked to perform an Easter program for American servicemen. They were then invited to perform in all the prisons of South Korea. Because the prisoners are so starved for entertainment, the players usually do a side-splitting comedy to show the prisoners that they have come as friends. Then comes the more serious part. The response of the prisoners as they applaud Jesus' rebuke of Satan, when Jesus

forgives the woman taken in adultery, when Lazarus is raised from
the dead, when Christ enters Jerusalem and when He appears after
His crucifixion is something the players will never forget. Lives
have been changed and warders are asking for more performances.
Not surprisingly, the troupe has been asked to perform in other
countries. (Ibid., 119)

The December 1981 newsletter of the World Association for Christian
Communication, *Action*, reported on a folk drama team based at Payap
University in Chiang Mai, Thailand. They used the traditional drama art
form of *ligay* to interpret biblical truths in ways that ordinary people could
understand. *Ligay* formed a bridge between Christian and non-Christian
people in the community. Many thousands of village people gathered to watch
these performances. The following is a report on how it began.

A missionary picked up a young girl named Kajorn who was hurt in
a bus accident when a piece of glass pierced her eye. The missionary
helped her during her recovery and she became a Christian, entering
Payap University in its first year. She came from a professional Thai
Folk Drama family. At Christmas she performed a Folk Drama for
entertainment. The missionary heard about it. He had wanted to use
Thai Folk Drama to communicate the Gospel when it was suggested
to him three years before by a bandit who said, "You stand up and
preach—that's Western. My people don't understand. If we tell the
stories in Folk Drama style they will understand." The missionary
and the young girl, with her father's help, produced their first drama,
"The Prodigal Daughter." From the first performance of the Ligay,
performed by Kajorn and the seminary students, the church never
let them stop.

Beginning with students, the troupe has grown to 25 professional
performers and staff. They give over 40 performances each dry
season (December through May) across Thailand.

God has chosen an art form held in low esteem, and is using it to
help people understand his plan of salvation in Christ. The Christian
Communications Institute of Payap University has helped change

people's image of Ligay by its use of skilled, educated actors and musicians, modern dramatic techniques, shortened performances, and clear, relevant messages. Audiences are drawn from all levels of society. Through the Ligay, people are touched by the depth and truth of the teachings of Jesus and can better understand God's grace.

Ligay performances serve to break down prejudices against the idea that Christianity is a Western religion only, and to open more and more hearts to Christ. God is using this common art form to bring the Gospel of Christ to every level of society. (Eubank 1989)

The use of drama presents its own particular set of problems and challenges as people seek to make it an effective tool of Christian ministry in an oral society. However, there is ample evidence to show that this is certainly being achieved. This should encourage us to take careful note of the drama forms that are being used in an oral culture and, if at all possible, to use them in the presentation of Christian truths to those people.

Case Study Strategy

- *Cultural context:* Christian message presented through indigenous drama forms. Message identified with local issues and cultural values.
- *Frame of reference:* Indigenous performers and scriptwriters understood their own culture and felt needs of their people.
- *Dynamic equivalence:* Scriptural message in indigenous dramatic form.
- *Performance and participation:* Audience responded in typical oral fashion, spontaneously and enthusiastically, during the drama presentation.
- *Oral communication skills:* Indigenous drama and songs. Drama groups formed from local Christian performers and musicians.
- *Biblical models:* Drama format followed biblical models and presented the message in a way that was easy to remember.

The Philippines: Singing, Dialogue, Questions

Keith Benn and his wife, Kathie, Australian members of WBT/SIL, began working among the Bontoc people of North Luzon, Philippines, in 1977. There were approximately twenty thousand Central Bontoc speakers living in some twenty villages of Mountain Province, and perhaps half that many again living and working outside the province. More than 50 percent of the young people (age fifteen to thirty) were literate, but perhaps less than 15 percent of the older adults had these skills. Approximately 75 percent of the Bontocs claimed to be bilingual in Ilocano, the trade language of the area, but their comprehension of Scripture in the second language was low.

At the suggestion of their literacy department, Keith and Kathie began writing scripts for Bible study cassettes for the Central Bontoc translations of Genesis 1–11 and James. They experimented with a number of different formats and worked through problems such as inadequate recording equipment and inappropriate people to do the reading. Gradually the length of Scripture reading was reduced, Western-style or unrelated hymns were removed, and the question-and-answer format became the main part in each presentation. The scripts used the following basic pattern:

1. Christian song
2. Introduction
3. Scripture reading
4. Bible study question
5. Instructions
6. Answer to question
7. Christian songs (songs may also be used throughout the program)

If a second question was asked about the same passage of Scripture, steps 4–6 were repeated.

Introduction. This is brief and tells what Scripture passage will now be read, outlining in perhaps a single sentence the theme of the passage.

Scripture readings. These are kept short (no more than ten verses); readings usually coincide with section headings of the translation. The Scripture readings are read by well-known and respected members of the community and leading representatives of the churches.

Bible study questions. Most of the questions asked are simple and straightforward, of the type used in translation checking. For example, "In what we have read here, what advice does James give for rich people?" The question is always repeated.

Instructions. The usual instruction is, "Now, turn the cassette recorder off, and look for the answer to the question." This instruction is followed by a five-second blank on the cassette. An alternative way of handling this instruction would be to state at the beginning of a cassette, "When you hear [any kind of instrument] play, turn off the cassette and look for the answer to the question."

Answers. Initially an answer may either be a direct quotation from the passage or a simple restatement of a verse, quoting the verse along with the answer. The answer may then also give a reference to other Scripture, quoting it and giving the reference. Answers, however, are kept brief.

Christian songs. The general plan was to prepare songs that reinforced the teaching of the passage under study. In some cases a theme was taken and expanded. In others, two or three verses were taken that summed up a theme, and these were rewritten to fit the structure of the syllable pattern of the indigenous tunes. These rewritten verses were then given to singers, who looked for indigenous tunes to fit the words. Many soloists and singing groups contributed to the musical portions of the tapes.

The following is a typical example of one of the cassette programs:

THEMATIC STUDIES IN THE GOSPEL OF LUKE: "LOVE YOUR ENEMIES"

Speaker 1 (a young man): Father, may I ask you something?
Speaker 2 (an older man): What is it, my child?
1: There is someone who slapped me. Because he is a big person I ran away, and now I have come to ask you, what should I do to take revenge against him?
2: If you take revenge, will that cause you to again be in harmony with him?
1: Perhaps not, father.
2: If you take revenge, will that help the peace or the pacification of trouble in the village?

1: It is true, my taking revenge will not help the welfare of the village. What should I do then?

2: What does God ("the One above") say we should do?

1: I do not know, father.

2: Let's read what Jesus said for us to do in the Gospel of Luke, chapter 6, from verse 27 to 31.

(Narrator reads Luke 6:27–31.)

2: Now, what does Jesus tell us to do to those who harm us? What advice does Jesus give if we have someone who causes us hardship?

(Study leader turns off cassette player and rereads Luke 6:27–31. Group looks for answer to the questions.)

(Song that paraphrases/reiterates teaching of Luke 6:27–31.)

It is important to notice how the dialogue script highlights some of the cultural values of an oral community; for instance, a young man learning from an older man, the importance of maintaining harmony in personal relationships, and the importance of the welfare of the group (the village). It is this sort of well-researched, carefully prepared script, as well as the appealing format, that creates the interest and holds the attention of the people in that community.

Threefold Goal

The Scripture on Cassette Program aimed to achieve a threefold goal: 1) to give oral people an opportunity to hear the Scripture; 2) to make a program so interesting that even non-church people would want to hear it; and 3) to provide the churches with a tool they would perceive to be of use. By 1985 there were more than forty-eight Bible study cassettes available, covering Scriptures from Genesis, Luke, Hebrews, James, and Thessalonians and also a range of topical questions. The more recently produced Bible study cassettes swept the Bontoc area like a bushfire. By the time of the missionaries' report, many hundreds of cassettes had been distributed to church leaders in each of the five denominations, and cassette Bible studies were underway in at least seventeen villages.

Some Responses to the Bible Study Cassettes

Two churches that had never found a place either for the printed Bontoc Scriptures or for Scripture on cassette began using the Bible studies in at least seven places. Roman Catholic priests who worked in a neighbouring dialect, which had far more translated Scripture than the Central dialect, started buying the Bontoc Scriptures and the new study cassettes out of their own pockets for use in Bible studies. Evangelists and village workers were given sets of tapes by their respective church leaders and sent into the mountains to begin Bible studies.

One church sent a missionary equipped with the cassettes and Scripture portions to a neighbouring language group. Six weeks later the pastor of the sending church visited him and baptized eleven new believers. An elder who had previously refused to help in making the cassettes accompanied the pastor on this visit and became quite enthusiastic about their value in evangelism.

Some folks from a Baptist church in Bontoc took the cassettes along when visiting a member in the local hospital. When they played the tape, twenty to thirty people gathered around to listen. They returned daily, expecting to terminate the study when their friend was discharged. But others asked to continue using the cassettes, and it was obvious that lives were being affected by the Scriptures in Bontoc.

> One evangelist testified, "I was always afraid to lead a Bible study before, but now it's easy. I just turn the cassette on, then when it asks a question, I stop it, and those present answer the question. Then I add some more teaching. When I have no more to say, I start the cassette again, and let the tape take over. Then after the next question, I add some more teaching. I'm not afraid any more. And do you know what? People are saying, 'Can you come to our house and hold a Bible study?' Now I'm run off my feet holding Bible studies in the places all around our village." (Benn 1985)

One exciting thing was that people who had never before led a Bible study now had regular studies in their homes. Ownership of a radio-cassette became a status symbol in the area, and many Bontocs who purchased tapes were also able to obtain their own recorder. Churches bought sets of cassettes for their uses.

Keys to Success

The following five factors contributed to the success of these Scripture cassettes:

Variety. Wherever possible, long sections of speaking were avoided, so that usually there were no more than three minutes without a break of some kind. To create breaks, sometimes hymns were inserted between question and answer or even in the middle of a Bible reading.

Indigenous music. In Bontoc there were some indigenous tunes that were unsuitable for hymns. What was suitable in one village was not necessarily acceptable in another. The tunes that were quite unacceptable were those too closely associated with sacrifice, death, and head-hunting.

One of the good things that came out of this presentation of Bible study cassettes was that church leaders started recognising that Bontoc people really did enjoy their own music. Comments such as "Wow, I never knew the Scripture was so clear!" or "When we hear the message using our own tunes, it comes through loud and clear!" help to reinforce the fact that indigenous music has a vital role in the communication process.

Church involvement. The Bible study cassettes were a community effort. Hymns from each of the four main churches were collected, and each church helped in the recording. Those who helped could now listen to the cassettes and hear their own hymns, which they had sung. These were scattered throughout the cassettes. In the recording, community leaders from three of the churches were also used. Those who helped in the recording were good ambassadors.

Thematic unity. The indigenous Christian songs used in the programs were either composed from the vernacular Bible verses used in the study or based upon the theme of the message. This helped to focus attention on the theme throughout the program and reinforced the teaching of the passage under study. For James more hymns were written than for Genesis, and they focused more directly on the message than did the Genesis ones, so there was better thematic continuity between the hymns and the Bible studies. For Luke about two hundred songs were recorded, which also were related directly to the studies.

A felt need. The cassettes came at a time when three of the churches had a felt need to hold Bible studies. Some people left the older established churches to be involved with the newer churches that were having Bible studies for their people. The Bible study cassettes were a tool that a variety of churches in Bontoc perceived to be of value. For the first time they were really using the translated Word (Benn 1985–86).

Case Study Strategy

Some case study strategy has been referred to in the analysis above, but the following is also important to note.

- *Cultural context:* Presentation made in vernacular. Messages set in local situation, highlighted cultural values, and identified with local issues.
- *Frame of reference:* Life involvement of expatriate missionaries. Understood indigenous communication forms and felt needs of the people.
- *Dynamic equivalence:* Scripture messages presented in the people's own language by means of dialogue, reading, discussion, and indigenous songs.
- *Group orientation:* Messages centred on group Bible studies and group discussion.
- *Performance and participation:* Question-and-answer technique used in the studies encouraged involvement of the whole group. Many different groups and individuals contributed to the indigenous Christian songs.

USING AUDIOCASSETTES IN ORAL SOCIETIES

As seen in some of the case studies described above, people have made very effective use of audiocassettes as a communication tool to be used with oral communicators. A special segment which deals with the use of audiocassettes and the production of relevant and effective cassette programs has been prepared in appendix 1. It also addresses some other technologies. Please refer to this if you are considering using audiocassettes or another technology in your communication strategy.

CONCLUSION

The above are just some examples of the way God has moved to make his message live in the cultures of oral peoples. But it has not happened by accident. As the case studies reveal, careful research was done, and patience and perseverance were needed, before the successful results were achieved. As the case study strategies also reveal, the communication principles set out in the previous chapters were the basis for the strategies employed, and as these were applied under the direction of the Holy Spirit, oral communicators responded in a positive way.

We move on now to apply these same principles to other very significant issues in oral societies: that of Christian leadership, and the place of literacy. These particular aspects of Christian ministry have their own challenges and success stories, but as we shall see, if these are approached in the right way, the response can be extremely worthwhile.

7

DEVELOPING CHRISTIAN LEADERSHIP IN ORAL SOCIETIES

Ole Kutengala is about fifty-five years old. In addition to his own language he speaks the national language and a neighbouring language as well. The district government, his sub-tribe and the churches in his area recognize him as one of the most influential Christian leaders among his people. His Christian maturity and wisdom are sought by local Christians and missionaries alike. However, his reading skills only qualify him to be called a semiliterate. He can not depend on his reading skills for his instruction.

Narendra Thotungal went to school through the third grade. He left school more than forty years ago. He has been too poor to buy books to continue developing his reading skill. He learned to "read" English, but speaks Hindi as his first language. . . . He can not read Hindi nor English well enough to understand government forms. However, he continues to serve as the key elder in his village church. He serves both as an evangelist and a principal adviser in the church.

Gonjaray initiated a Bible study in her home. It grew into a small congregation with her determined leadership. In spite of opposition at home and in the community as well as being unable to read, the congregation at her house has grown strong. (Elliston 1988b, 1)

The need to develop Christian leadership in oral societies is clearly evident in many areas around the world. It is particularly evident in developing countries, where the church is growing rapidly and where present training institutions and programs are just not keeping pace with the demand for effective leadership. The Cape Town Commitment states clearly,

> The majority of the world's population are oral communicators, who cannot or do not learn through literate means, and more than half of them are among the unreached. . . .
>
> As we recognize and take action on issues of orality, let us:
>
> a. Make greater use of oral methodologies in discipling programmes, even among literate believers.
> b. Make available an oral format Story Bible in the heart languages of unreached and unengaged people groups as a matter of priority.
> c. Encourage mission agencies to develop oral strategies, including: the recording and distribution of oral Bible stories for evangelism, discipling and leadership training, along with appropriate orality training for pioneer evangelists and church-planters; these could use fruitful oral and visual communication methods for communicating the whole biblical story of salvation, including storytelling, dances, arts, poetry, chants and dramas.
> d. Encourage local churches in the Global South to engage with unreached people groups in their area through oral methods that are specific to their worldview.
> e. Encourage seminaries to provide curricula that will train pastors and missionaries in oral methodologies. (Third Lausanne Congress 2011, II.D.2)

Unfortunately many churches and missions still feel that when it comes to leadership training, the Western, literacy-oriented, formal training system is the only one that will produce the "right" sort of leaders. In this chapter I will attempt to move beyond formal, literacy-oriented training and consider the "creative local initiatives" available in oral communities that can provide the basis for the development of effective Christian leadership within those communities.

In this chapter the focus is on training Christian leaders. This is developed in relation to the proposition that oral, event-oriented communication techniques that are part of a people's own culture are the most appropriate ones to use in training oral people to become Christian leaders in their society. This chapter is also used to highlight the fact that oral communicators will not be any less effective than literates simply because they have not come through the formal, literacy-oriented system. In fact the reverse will be the case.

LEADERSHIP PATTERNS OF ORAL COMMUNICATORS

Having considered the characteristics of oral, event-oriented cultures, it naturally follows that the leadership patterns within those cultures will be shaped by those characteristics—not that it is possible to present a single idea of what constitutes nonliterate leadership, as each culture will have its own model. Even by looking at one specific group, it is difficult to see exactly what marks out a person as a leader for that group. However, by considering the cultural characteristics that oral peoples have in common, we can highlight some of the features that influence the shaping of their leadership. This then helps us not only in discerning the true leadership of such societies, but also in determining how Christian leadership can be developed most effectively among them.

ORAL LEADERSHIP CHARACTERISTICS

A leader in an oral society will be *event oriented*, and as such will be involved in the events of his or her own community. Western-oriented mission personnel or church leaders may bypass such people as leaders because they "never turn up on time" to church meetings, but this could very well be because of their participation in community events until those are completed. They will operate in an event-oriented time frame.

A nonliterate leader will demonstrate skill in the various ways used by the oral community to gain and preserve knowledge. These skills will vary of course with each culture, but if the person is a leader, they will be accomplished in at least some of those skills, and they will have a good memory. They will have a clear knowledge of the values and traditions of the culture and know how to teach them to others.

As indicated by many of the characteristics, a nonliterate leader will be *group oriented*, seeking to promote cooperation and harmony within the cultural group rather than pressing for competition and superior attainment by individuals. Because of this characteristic, leaders in oral cultures may not be prominent as individuals. They simply do not promote themselves as individuals, nor do they want other people to promote them as such. Leaders in these communities may have distinct personalities and clear leadership qualities and be accomplished in their cultural leadership skills, but they will not usually "stand out" as individuals. In fact, they probably view individual prominence as a bad character trait and seek to avoid it.

Don McGregor, a missionary in Papua New Guinea, tells the tragic story of a man who by dint of much hard work and personal effort became a prominent man in his own community. He was eventually elected as the local member for the national parliament in Port Moresby and as such received a cash salary that made him a wealthy person in comparison to his own people. He fulfilled his clan obligations to the tune of hundreds of dollars, but still kept the greater portion of the money for himself and acquired things for himself such as a sawn-timber house, a tractor, a number of head of cattle, and a trade store. At the next election he won only a handful of votes, and it became known in his area that people did not want to vote for such a selfish man. Rejected by his people, this man became sick with bronchial pneumonia. He gave away lots of money to try and restore harmony with his people and also with his ancestral spirits. But in spite of frantic efforts with traditional healing rituals, and also Western medicine, he eventually died. The meaning of his death was very clear to everyone—he was too selfish and had too much authority. After that it was difficult to get people to stand as candidates for election to the parliament (McGregor 1982, 78).

A nonliterate leader will be *conservative* in outlook because of the high regard for tradition and, although open to change, will usually be cautious about seeing it happen. The moral, social, and religious values of a nonliterate society will be exemplified in its leaders. In other words, they will be models that other people can observe and imitate if they wish to become people whose lives are in harmony with the ideals of their culture.

> Among the Maasai several words are used to designate a leader. One of the most common words is *olaiguanani* which comes from the verb which means to discuss. The leader then is the one who can listen and discuss an issue in a way which puts it into historical context, puts everyone's ideas into the context and gives structure to a

group consensus. (Elliston 1988a, 12; see also ch. 5, Hovey's example from Papua New Guinea of leadership skills being demonstrated through consensus in decision making)

LEADERS AND FOLLOWERS

Leadership is not just a matter that relates to one person, or a number of individuals, but followers are a very significant part of the leadership process.

> Leadership is a process, not a person, although it depends on a leader's legitimacy. Certainly, the leader is the central and often the vital part of the leadership process. However, the followers are also important in the picture. Without responsive followers there is no leadership, because the concept of leadership is relational. It involves someone who exerts influence, and those who are influenced. However, influence can flow both ways. People other than the leader, and the nature of the social setting in which they relate to one another, are also necessary parts of leadership. (Hollander 1978, 4)

This is very evident in the oral community context, where leaders are sensitive to group concerns and are looking to the group for support and approval. But the group also has a very strong influence on the leader and is able to apply group pressure to ensure that group values are maintained.

PROBLEMS FACED BY LEADERS WHO ARE ORAL COMMUNICATORS

Over the last two centuries missions has taken the message of Christianity to every area of the world, and the result has been a dramatic increase in the establishment and growth of Christian churches. The presentation of the gospel and the subsequent teaching of converts has for the most part followed the Western pattern of preaching and teaching, and the strong emphasis of missions has been to make Christians literate so that they can use the Western formal education system to become spiritually mature. In general, it has been mission and church policy to choose leaders who are literate and who have formal educational qualifications.

This emphasis then establishes a cycle whereby those leaders who are chosen will in turn choose leaders with similar literacy-oriented qualifications. In many cases the national church leaders who have been chosen in this way are even more eager to promote the same system than the expatriates who introduced it. The oral leadership skills and leadership qualifications recognised by an oral community are either not known or not recognised by the missions and churches working amongst them. As a result the people in those communities, who are influenced by the mission or church, come to perceive their oral skills and concepts as somehow inferior to the literacy-oriented system.

For nonliterate leaders in an oral community this has brought many problems, and even if they have accepted the gospel, the introduction of the Western communication and education system has had some damaging, far-reaching effects. It will be helpful here if we consider some of the comments of researchers who have worked in this particular area of concern. Klem presents insights from the context of Africa:

> The missionary emphasis on literacy and Western schooling was founded on two basic assumptions. The first was that African culture was basically so evil that it could never become a vehicle for adequately expressing Christian truth. Therefore young people had to be extracted from the culture of their birth and trained in a distinctly Godly or Western environment. There was not much hope of an authentic Christianization of the adults who could not be separated from their indigenous culture.

> The second assumption was that the most valuable and important information Christians should know is to be learned from books by reading. Only comparatively modern Western modes of communication are suited to the expression of Christian truth. This was assumed because we perceived in the Scriptures only one acceptable method of teaching. We lacked the cultural exposure to realize that people are perfectly capable of learning and teaching many things without depending upon books. (1982, 33)

Klem gives a graphic illustration of the effects of the mission/church policy of literacy on nonliterate leaders. He quotes a story from McGavran, who observed an older Nigerian man in a church meeting pretending to find the correct page and number in a hymnbook, using the book to sing all the words of the hymn, but failing to realize that he was holding the book upside down!

> What must be the inner confusion and loss of self-esteem of a mature man who feels motivated to play such a charade. How inwardly debilitating must be the sense of not actually having skill for the role he feels he ought to play but cannot. It is, furthermore, a great devaluation of such a man's memory skill to feel it necessary to sing the hymn hiding behind a mask of false literacy. Such men and women have all the potential for genuine Bible knowledge and Christian maturity if literacy were not considered the only gateway to it. (Ibid., 38–39)

Klem also points out the detrimental effects literacy has had on the cultural patterns of leadership. Historically in oral communities, recognized leaders were those who had gained maturity in age and experience, who had a retentive memory, and who demonstrated skill in using the proverbs of the tribe. But because the church has relied heavily on using literate communication as the primary method of teaching Scripture and Christian doctrine, the indigenous leadership structures have been challenged and displaced by recognising as leaders people who have literacy-oriented qualifications.

With the introduction of literacy, recognition and power were given to the young people who did well in school work, where reading is all-important. Often, however, the young people came back from school not knowing the stories and oral art of their people. They lacked many of the traditional requirements for leadership. Yet in the modern scheme of things, the young were frequently given positions of administrative authority over their elders since the latter could not read (ibid., 39–40).

Ted Ward gives account of some of the problems faced by adults who have only known a nonformal education system, such as those in oral societies, and who are faced with the option of either learning through a foreign, formal system or relinquishing their previous leadership roles. The formal education system is rigid and demanding and seems incapable of adjusting to the needs of those who are unable to cope with the abstract, complex mental processes assumed by that system to be the basis of any valuable learning experience.

Lacking an educational process which will reach him at his level, the informally learned individual will almost certainly experience a high degree of frustration and failure in the schools and will either opt out or be shut out of the formally sanctioned schooling system. In effect, he will be excluded from access to social credentials and relegated to personal poverty, powerlessness, and social unproductiveness.

> It is clearly absurd to expect a 40-year-old illiterate peasant to possess the same cognitive processes and to have the same needs and concerns as a child of an urban, middle class family. Yet this has been precisely the assumption upon which most formal education systems have operated. (Ward and Herzog 1974, 26, 27, 33)

Harvie Conn writes about the effects of Western cultural presuppositions on the teaching of missions and evangelism in the Majority World, and lists some as:

> The equation of learning with schooling: Institutionalism.
> The equation of professionalism with ministry: Elitism.
> The equation of theorization with knowledge: Abstractionism.
> (1984, 250–59)

The following is an extract from his comments on the last of these, as he describes the reaction of a nonliterate Christian leader when discussing the Western-oriented, formal education Bible school training that was available in his area:

> "I never know what to say when people object to me about Christianity; I always feel ignorant. I just talk about who Jesus is in the Bible and what he has done for me. But I wish I could go to school and really learn how to do evangelism."

> Behind these proverbial formulations and situations lies the given of western abstractionism, the equation of acquiring theories with acquiring "knowledge." Abstractionism is not an assault on the development of theories or the teaching of theories. It is the hidden presumption that, in developing and learning them, we have found reality. (Ibid.)

The above comments help us to understand just how pervasive is the influence of Western cultural presuppositions in developing countries, and how difficult it is for people to break away from them and to regain confidence in their own cultural systems. The Christian leader in the example quoted above, because of his presuppositions about a Western-oriented training program, did not perceive, nor is he likely to be encouraged to do so, that his simple personal testimony—"I just talk about who Jesus is in the Bible and what he has done for me"—is probably one of the most effective means of communication he could use.

The nonliterate leader who wants to have a place in the Western-oriented church leadership structure faces the prospect of completely transforming the learning aspects of his worldview so that he can comprehend the formal instruction program he will have to undertake in order to become qualified as a teacher, or some other type of recognised leader. He will then have to learn a completely new set of skills in order to be able to teach the material he has learned and to carry out any other leadership responsibilities. He will also have to be prepared to accept a leadership role assigned to him by people from outside his own community, one which will probably place him under the authority and supervision of younger men. It is not so surprising then that many nonliterate leaders prefer to opt out of such a system and not become involved at all in the Christian church.

TRAINING NONLITERATE CHRISTIAN LEADERS

Even a brief examination, as we have made above, of the problems facing nonliterate Christian leaders who would like to be a vital part of their church's ministry makes the task seem very difficult indeed. But the main bulk of the work that needs to be done is by the people and groups who are in positions of authority and responsibility with regard to the selection and training of such people. This is where major changes must be made if nonliterate leaders are going to be able to contribute their full potential to the church. Modern research in this area appears to point in one direction, and that is that teaching and learning skills need to be carefully matched, oriented to the learner and his or her context.

In this connection, Ward defines two categories of education, formal and nonformal. The nonformal, which also includes unplanned, informal instruction, has proved to be by far the most effective style of education. This is the area of instruction that would be appropriate for the nonliterate adult.

The non-schooled adult is not always unlearned or uneducated. Large amounts of knowledge relating to social and economic life have been learned through word-of-mouth transmission and through modelling. Social roles, agricultural and construction skills, crafts, history, language, and so forth, are passed on from generation to generation through an informal but often highly refined system of informal learning. Whether the learning takes place through informal tutoring, supervised on-the-job training, apprenticeship or by listening to stories and legends recounted by elders, the informally learned individual is primarily discovery-oriented and is usually operating at a concrete level of mental operations. (Ward and Herzog 1974, 26–27)

In other words, the person learning through the informal system looks for answers to the concrete problems of their everyday life and experience. Their success is gauged by the real and immediate rewards of physical health through the provision of food, clothing, and shelter, as well as social acceptance and well-being, rather than the abstract, academic awards of grades and certificates. Success therefore encourages reinforcement and retention of the material learned. The whole learning situation is directly related to the concrete reality of the learner's life and experience.

To explain briefly, *formal education* refers to the system that is well known in Western society, which is highly structured, curriculum oriented, usually conducted in an educational institution, and generally rather inflexible. It is governed by an educational body that is given authority and recognition by the society. *Nonformal education*, on the other hand, usually operates outside the classroom, in a more flexible setting. It is person centred and focuses on practical uses of knowledge. *Informal education* refers to the learning that takes place in the learner's natural social environment. It is usually unplanned and is the type of situation and learning style that is best suited to nonliterate adults, both for learning and teaching.

It is sufficient to say here that when considering a training program for nonliterate leaders, it is most important to use appropriate learning styles. If the training program we use with nonliterate leaders promotes learning styles that are in contrast to natural oral styles, then we should not be surprised if progress in leadership development is slow. In relation to the training of nonliterate Christian leaders, there are certain guidelines we will consider that are connected with the worldview of nonliterates, and which are essential for any planned curriculum.

Treat Nonliterate Learners as Adults

Make sure learners are given the respect and recognition that they would normally receive in their own place of living. Also expect them to learn on an adult level consistent with their own cultural experience. Teachers assigned to instruct nonliterate adults should be appropriate. Younger people or women, especially single women, may not be regarded with the respect or credibility normally given to teachers in their own community. They may also be looking for adult communication forms, quite distinct from those used with children or young people.

> It may be that the instructor will have to learn some new ways to teach adults. For example, among the Maasai of Kenya mature adults expect to learn from other mature adults through the use of proverbs. The Amharas of Ethiopia expect levels of subtlety and related double meanings to be present with adult teachers. (Elliston 1988a, 20)

We can conclude, then, that it is very important to discover the adult communication forms that are in an oral society and determine their suitability for incorporation into a Christian leadership training program.

Encourage Participation

Participation should be encouraged not only in the learning and teaching sessions, but also in the planning and evaluation of the program. This fits their worldview pattern, makes them feel the program is theirs, and also ensures relevance in the course content. A skilled instructor will also make sure that through participation the experience and wisdom of the people are contributed as a valuable part of the course.

A most valuable study has been prepared by Robert Primrose dealing with the whole program of bringing nonliterate people through to spiritual maturity without them learning to read (Primrose 1976). In his final summary he outlines a number of patterns of interaction that he regards as essential in the process of effective communication and learning by nonliterates. These correspond to the focus on participation, which I have mentioned, and are particularly applicable to this issue of training nonliterate Christian leaders.

Consider the Cultural Time Frame

For most oral communicators the time frame chosen for a training program will be most significant and will certainly affect who can participate. For those in rural or coastal areas away from the towns, seasonal conditions must be taken into account. Time of day, day (or days) of the week, and length of the course will also be important. In urban areas too there will be many nonliterates, and instructors must allow for the fact that promptness and punctuality are not treasured values among them.

Contextualize the Course Content

The basis for the course content of any Christian leadership training program should always be the Scriptures, but the issues that are dealt with need to be related to the people's cultural values and everyday experiences. Some of the issues will be new; for example, "loving your enemies" may be a totally new concept, but it needs to be presented in terms that are familiar and that concrete relational thinkers can understand.

From an oral perspective, words are much more than phonological symbols; they are directly related to people, events, and power, and as such, any messages that are presented to nonliterates must be very carefully prepared. Choice of vocabulary is most important, as abstract terms and concepts and religious jargon must be avoided. Terms that are used should be action and event oriented, and ones that are believable and explainable in relation to present-day activities. Contextualization of the message is even more essential in oral contexts than in literate ones; hearers must be able to relate the message to what is known and understood. Oral people are not used to guessing and hypothesizing what a speaker might be meaning.

Even if the speaker is fluent in the vernacular, because of the spiritual nature of the messages, we cannot expect that the receptors will make precise interpretations. We have to build up images that, when they are all put together, say what we mean. Truth in the abstract is not a relevant concept in most oral cultures; what is true is if it resonates with their context and past. If two things match their experience, they have no trouble holding them together, even if for literate people the combination is not logically possible (see Wiseman 1987a, 37–38).

The teaching will always have to be considered in the context of its presentation, and that will include the person doing the presentation. In Australia, among the Aborigines, even non-Christians will not listen to a Christian message if they feel that the speaker is either not qualified (by knowledge and experience) or that his or her personal testimony does not match the message.

Use Communication Forms that Are Appropriate

This will be considered in fuller detail in chapter 9. At this point it is sufficient to emphasise that communication forms are extremely important in oral societies, and a training program for leaders in such a society must give top priority to using communication forms that are appropriate and effective.

Provide Material that Is Structured for Remembrance

Keep in mind the scriptural precedents discussed in chapters 3 and 4, where it was shown that the vast bulk of the Scriptures, in both the Old and New Testaments, were presented in a variety of communicational forms that facilitated their oral remembrance. In training Christian leaders in oral communities, we need to have the same goals. Relevant Scripture texts, catechisms, and other Christian material can be prepared in the local communication forms and given to the trainee leaders to commit to memory. Failure to incorporate this methodology into a training program for Christian leaders is to neglect a marvellous and very relevant communication skill that has already been provided within the trainee leaders themselves and also within the whole community.

SCRIPTURAL PRECEDENTS FOR DEVELOPING NONLITERATE LEADERSHIP

During the period of history encompassed by the record of Scripture, the Israelite people were primarily an oral society. The Scriptures give us many examples of how nonliterate leadership was developed among these people, and all of them would be relevant to consider in connection with this study. However, it will suffice if we focus on the most prominent of these examples, that of Jesus developing leadership among his disciples.

As indicated previously (ch. 3), Jesus chose to reject the methods of the scholars and the wealthy educated class, and used instead the contemporary, oral vernacular tradition of the common people. Jesus' communication was down-to-earth, people centred, and related to concrete situations and everyday life. As we consider his communicational techniques and his commitment to his disciples and the common people, we realize that he presents us with the ultimate model of communicating to oral people and also of developing effective leadership in an oral community.

Jesus' Model of Leadership

Jesus taught his disciples in a way that was most appropriate for oral people, and he developed their leadership potential in a culturally appropriate way also—he modelled leadership for them. Jesus used a combination of discipleship and apprenticeship techniques in what has been described as "life involvement" (C. Kraft 1983, 46; see also the discussion of this term in ch. 5) to present this model of leadership to them. We will highlight here three prominent features of that multifaceted model.

The Servant Model

Jesus regarded himself as a servant. He knew he had been sent by his Father, but sent to be a servant, and he made this abundantly clear to his disciples by means of parable, illustrations, and graphic example.

> The kings of the Gentiles lord it over them; and those who exercise authority over them call themselves Benefactors. But you are not to be like that. Instead, the greatest among you should be like the youngest, and the one who rules like the one who serves. For who is greater, the one who is at the table or the one who serves? Is it not the one who is at the table? But I am among you as one who serves. (Luke 22:25–27)

During the "Last Supper," his final meeting with his disciples before his crucifixion, he washed his disciples' feet, a task usually performed only by servants.

You call me "Teacher" and "Lord," and rightly so, for that is what I am. Now that I, your Lord and Teacher, have washed your feet, you also should wash one another's feet. I have set you an example that you should do as I have done for you. Very truly I tell you, no servant is greater than his master, nor is a messenger greater than the one who sent him. Now that you know these things, you will be blessed if you do them. (John 13:13–17)

It seems that the secular and religious milieu of Christ's time presented many of the same problems that Christians face today. The models and principles of leadership displayed there had a strong influence on the disciples, and as far as Jesus was concerned, they were the very opposite of what he had in mind.

Paul also perceived Jesus' role during his ministry on earth to be that of a servant, and described it very graphically to the Philippians in the course of exhorting them to live out this same role.

In your relationships with one another, have the same mindset as Christ Jesus:

Who, being in very nature God,
did not consider equality with God something to be used to
his own advantage;
rather, he made himself nothing
by taking the very nature of a servant,
being made in human likeness.
And being found in appearance as a man,
he humbled himself
by becoming obedient to death—even death on a cross!
(Phil 2:5–8)

Through this model, Jesus established once and for all that the essence of spiritual leadership is service (see Elliston 1988b).

The Shepherd Model

John chapter 10 gives us a concise summary of Jesus' perception of the shepherd model, but throughout his ministry Jesus demonstrated what a shepherd leader is like and impressed this upon his disciples. The following are some of the features of shepherd leadership:

- The shepherd knows the sheep (John 10:3,14,15,28). He calls them by name. This is not just a superficial knowledge, but a deep understanding.
- He is always with them (John 10:3,4,28). The shepherd is right there among the sheep, not just overseeing them at a distance. It is not a come-and-go ministry.
- He leads the sheep (John 10:3,4,27). He leads them in the right direction, and also provides their food and drink.
- He protects the sheep (John 10:10–15). He is watchful for the dangers that could harm the sheep and prepared to be involved personally in protecting the sheep.
- He is prepared to die for the sheep (John 10:11,15). He is completely committed to the sheep and values the welfare of the sheep above his own life.
- He is concerned for the lost sheep (Matt 9:36–38; 18:12; John 10:16). The shepherd has a vision for outreach to those who have deliberately wandered away, as well as to those who are not yet part of the flock.

The Steward Model

The "steward" refers to someone who is appointed as a manager or trustee of some valuable property or important undertaking. During his earthly ministry, Jesus was very conscious of the responsibility he had to bring the word of God to the people of God and to prepare trained leaders to take that word into all the world. He also knew he had to impart to those people that same responsibility of stewardship. He continually reminded the disciples of the privilege that was theirs as recipients of his teaching, and that with that privilege was the implication of responsibility and obligation. He told parables and stories to impress upon these fledgling leaders that they would be accountable for their privileges and positions of trust. He lived the model of stewardship in front of them every day, and in the prayer to his Father recorded in John 17 we can discern the sense of satisfaction and achievement at having carried out the assigned task:

> I have revealed you to those whom you gave me out of the world . . .
> and they have obeyed your word. . . . I gave them the words you gave
> me and they have accepted them. They knew with certainty that I
> came from you, and they believed that you sent me. . . .
>
> . . . As you sent me into the world, I have sent them into the world.
> (vv. 6,8,18)

The themes of *servanthood, shepherding,* and *stewardship* are very neatly integrated in Peter's exhortation to leaders of the early church:

> Be *shepherds* of God's flock that is under your care, watching over
> them—not because you must, but because you are willing, as God
> wants you to be; not pursuing dishonest gain, but *eager to serve*;
> not lording it over those *entrusted* to you, but being *examples* to the
> flock. (1 Pet 5:2,3, emphasis mine)

These models of servant, shepherd, and steward can be most helpful in the training of nonliterate leaders, provided of course that the concepts portrayed through those models are appropriate and clearly discernible within a given cultural context (see Elliston 1988b).

TOWARD A STRATEGY FOR DEVELOPING CHRISTIAN LEADERS IN ORAL SOCIETIES

The Christian church today is experiencing unprecedented growth in countries around the world. Congregations are expanding and new churches are being planted at a much faster rate than leaders can be trained to look after them. The churches with the greatest needs are in developing countries where the majority of the people are oral communicators.

As outlined in the study above, it *is* possible to develop effective nonliterate leadership, and this is within the capacity of the churches within those countries. However, if nonliterate leadership is going to be developed to a point where it is effective in providing teaching and pastoral care for the church and evangelism for the community, then there has to be a change in approach on the part of those responsible for the selection, training, and appointment of leaders. These people need to realize that training programs for leaders, as well as the regular activities and outreach of the local churches, must become oriented towards the oral perspective of the people concerned. Some specific suggestions as to how this might be done are indicated in the sections above.

In speaking about nonformal education, Elliston quotes Ward, who has some appropriate comments to make in relation to this issue. Ward outlines four basic reasons why this kind of educational approach is valid for the church that is developing in an oral society.

> The first argument is *historical* deriving from the example of the training ministry of Jesus Christ and from the recurrences of his procedures as exemplified, for example, in Martin Luther and John Wesley. It is no accident that Jesus used a nonformal approach to the development of his disciples. . . .

> The second argument is *demographical*. . . . There are three demographical factors that must be worked into the formula for cost-effective pastoral education: *geographical*, in the sense of where the pastors are versus where the theological school is; *economic*, in the sense of support for the pastor-in-training and his family; and *sociological*, in the matter of what sort of persons are attracted, how much of what sorts of previous education and experience of what sort of cultural background a person must have in order to fit into the life of the school. . . .

> The third argument for the extension approach is *theological*. It is necessary to consider not only who does come into a training program, but who should come. If the purpose is to train people so that they might become pastors, that is quite different. . . .

> The fourth argument is *pedagogical*. This can be summarised by saying that an emphasis on clinical field experience and an emphasis on continuing education, reflects the growing recognition that professional training is a life-long endeavour (Ward and Herzog 1974, 248). (Elliston 1988a, 29–31)

To add just a little to the historical argument mentioned by Ward, in relation to nonliterate people, the biblical precedents are very significant. As we examine both the Old and New Testament models of leadership, we find that it is not a matter of rank or status, or dominant control, which are the features of normal secular leadership today. In fact, Jesus' strongest criticisms were levelled at that type of leadership. Rather we see the constantly recurring theme of servanthood, and also in Paul's writings, the emphasis on the total contribution of the body of Christ for the purpose of mutual edification and strengthening of the local church. There is no mention that dominant leadership roles are required at all. Elliston's statement is appropriate in this connection: "Let the church then train leaders who can serve" (1988b, 31).

To sum up, a strategy for the development of Christian leaders in oral societies will include the following: 1) An in-depth understanding of the oral skills and capabilities appropriate to leaders in that oral society. 2) An in-depth understanding of the learning styles and information preservation techniques used by the society, especially in the development of its leaders. Performance and participation are key elements in this understanding. 3) An in-depth understanding of the communication forms used by the society, and which ones are most appropriate for leadership development.

Determining the above will require careful research, and this will also be an ongoing exercise. A leadership program can then be developed that will incorporate all of the above and will also introduce people to the leadership models demonstrated by Jesus. The program should also aim for minimal cultural dislocation.

At this point, it would be appropriate if we considered some case studies of contemporary situations that utilize some of the principles mentioned above.

SOME CONTEMPORARY CASE STUDIES

Papua New Guinea

As mentioned previously (see ch. 6), Hovey used the concept of a genealogy stick, along with the traditional communication forms of discussion and storytelling, to communicate the Christian message to Papua New Guineans. Hovey found that this method was also very effective in developing leadership among the newly converted nonliterates. With the older men especially, it was important that they gain confidence in knowing the Bible stories. Some extracts from his paper on training nonliterate church leaders will help us to understand some of the problems he faced and just how a satisfactory level of success was achieved.

> In the past I had tried to encourage older men to take a leadership role in the services, but without success. It seems that the reason for them not doing so is the importance of stories, legends and myths in the PNG culture. Great prestige is afforded a man who knows a lot of these stories, as these stories are really the title deeds to much that they consider to be real property, i.e., land rights, the rights to the use of clan names, access to ancestors, etc. . . . As a result a man who doesn't know the background stories of a particular matter would never consider taking a leading role in the exercise of that matter. Consequently, these older men would feel terribly ashamed taking a leadership role in services unless they knew the stories, in this case, Bible stories that would give them the necessary background. . . .

> To further enhance the learning of these stories, we spent the evenings during the course in one of three activities. The first was dramatization of the story learnt during the day, the second was to have the men divide into their language groups (7 in all) and retell the stories among themselves in their languages, using the shared story-telling style which they use in all story telling in their villages except in story debates. As a third, we had men from each group tell legends from their own villages which covered similar material. Apart from the benefits that exposure to these legends was to myself, comparing them to Bible stories did raise important theological differences to the level of consciousness so that they could begin to be dealt with. Also the effect of two way sharing on the subject heightened the communication impact of these stories.

> In the class on Bible stories, we did not teach interpretation with the stories. As much interpretation as was taught, was taught in a very practical class on Christian living. In this we dealt with many areas of PNG felt needs, especially those dealing with the spirit world. Wherever possible, the Bible stories already learnt were used to get across the point in this teaching. By doing it this way we were able

to follow traditional use of their own stories which are referred to when discussing certain types of behaviour, and then points from the stories are applied to condemn or condone the behaviour being discussed. I guess this was our theology class, but it was designed to be lived, not just learnt. As traditional education and communication techniques have been used for centuries to develop moral values, it seems more than appropriate that the church which is aiming for the same ends should also use the same methods. (1980, 6, 7, 9)

It is amazing to see how effective the oral communication techniques are when they are put into practice, as in the case study above. Once we can get away from the literacy-oriented, monologue, formal teaching situation, then there is the opportunity for genuine interaction, and learning takes place with all who are involved, including both teachers and students (see also Primrose 1976, 33–40). As oral people see that their own learning and communication system is being recognised and affirmed, so they become enthusiastic about using it to express and teach their Christian faith, which helps them to grow in their knowledge of Christian things and in their confidence to be able to teach them to others. So a marvellous cycle of increasing spiritual growth and ability is established, which should be evaluated and encouraged.

Australia

I have described the use of iconographs, drama, and singing in communicating the Christian message to the Warlpiri people of Central Australia (ch. 2). These media of communication began to be used more and more in the area of teaching theology to indigenous Christian leaders. Regular teaching sessions started taking place, and little by little nonliterate leaders accumulated a valuable store of Christian teaching that not only strengthened and enriched their own lives but which they were able to pass on to others. This sort of teaching has been given the title of "gum-leaf theology." But this was not achieved lightly. Much intensive preparation was made to ensure that the teaching material met the criteria for effective communication: relevant, clearly comprehensible, interesting, and making use of appropriate symbols.

Details from a training course report will help us to understand how these techniques were used to develop nonliterate leadership.

The last two courses have centred around an iconograph (Aboriginal style symbolic drawing). The drawing contains each of the points contained in the teaching of the subject being presented. It also contains a number of concise statements in English.

As the course proceeds, each point is taught from the drawing. This is a big help to the ones who are unable to read very much, and is much more meaningful than the printed page. The statements in English are helps for the readers.

At the end of the course, each successful student receives a copy of the teaching cloth (on which is printed the iconograph). It is both a reward for success and a very useful preaching aid. The idea of the course is to provide material for the student to pass on to his church.

Back in their communities, the students begin working on the statements. They are translated into their own languages—Warlpiri, Gurinji, and Alyawarra. This reinforces the teaching, and provides basic preaching points.

The next step is the composition of songs based on these translated statements. The songs are set to traditional style chants, and are therefore highly relevant to all who hear them.

Once the songs are composed, a full scale Christian corroboree can be organized, with symbolic action, mime and body painting combining with the songs to provide a unique and powerful means of conveying Scriptural truth. (Whitbourne 1984; see also Ollerenshaw 1986)

These media of communication used in the Aboriginal cultural context have had a marked impact on the whole community in that area. It has gradually affected a wider and wider circle of contacts and hopefully will encourage other groups with different cultural forms of oral communication to use those forms for the expression and teaching of their Christian faith.

CONCLUSION

For an issue such as the development of nonliterate Christian leadership, a fully comprehensive treatment is not possible in a study such as the above. However, the thrust of this chapter has been to underscore the fact that nonliterate societies have perfectly adequate systems of communication for training, and that it is a very viable proposition to undertake a leadership development program in oral societies without having to base it on literacy or Western education philosophy and techniques.

The striking example of which we can constantly remind ourselves is that of Jesus himself. In the context of an oral society, he did not use books or a literacy-oriented program, but deliberately chose the oral communication system of that society to teach the people who were to become the first leaders of his church.

The tragedies Western missionaries must be aware of and aim to avoid are, firstly, producing Christian leaders who are merely clones of Western, literacy-oriented leadership, and who have only minimal potential to provide effective Christian teaching and leadership for their oral communities; and secondly, overlooking people who are true leaders in their community and thereby failing to lead them on to mature Christian leadership, or by the nature of the training program, eliminating such people from effective leadership positions in their Christian community. Every context will be different and may present many more problems than have been addressed in the study above. However, if we keep in mind the principle of receptor orientation, and acknowledge the presence of and our constant dependence upon the Holy Spirit, then there is every possibility that our involvement in the development of Christian leadership among oral communicators will prove successful.

In the next chapter careful consideration is given to a crucial issue in the development of a communication strategy to oral societies that will be both effective and realistic. It is especially crucial in the light of internal and external pressures being brought to bear on such societies to have a meaningful place in the modern world. That issue is the place of literacy in an oral society.

8

THE PLACE OF LITERACY IN ORAL SOCIETIES

INTRODUCTION

Our focus in this book is on oral communicators and all that is involved in achieving effective communication of the Christian message to them, especially in terms of their own oral communication systems. However, there are very few oral communities in the world where the effect of literacy and the formal education systems of the modern Western-oriented world have not been felt. In many cases the effects have been major, and as such directly affect whatever considerations we may make about the communication system of an oral society and any communication strategy we may use for presenting the Christian message to them. So while stressing the importance of understanding and using the oral communication context of these societies, we cannot afford to ignore literacy as a very relevant issue in their midst. This chapter seeks to briefly address some of the issues relating to literacy in an oral society and to suggest some possibilities of a literacy program that would be effective and relevant in such a society.

PERCEPTION OF LITERACY BY ORAL SOCIETIES

It is extremely difficult for anyone coming from a context of literacy, literature, and Western-oriented formal education to understand clearly how literacy is perceived by oral societies (Ong 1982, 31). But it should be carefully noted that the perception of literacy by oral societies is usually markedly different from the way literates perceive it. The basis for this difference is in the worldview of these different societies, and in particular the cognitive processes of the people within them. This has been discussed in some detail in chapters 5–7. However, intellectual knowledge of these differences often does not prepare a literate person for the shock of just how great those differences are.

Margaret Wendell mentions a number of these different perceptions as she seeks to prepare eager literacy teachers for some possibly unexpected revelations. Basic to a lot of misunderstanding of literacy by oral communicators is the perception that it is foreign and therefore does not necessarily "make sense" or appear relevant to their society. Some of the perceptions that Wendell mentions include the following (1982, 8):

Literacy brings prestige. This is usually associated with literacy in the national language or a prestigious foreign language such as English or French. People with such perceptions often would not see the need for learning to read their own vernacular—after all, they already know that. But they believe that in order to learn another language and gain the prestige that comes with that, they would have to learn to read that language.

Literacy means Christianity. Because Christian missions has been so closely linked with schooling and literacy, and in some communities Christians are the only people with books and literacy skills, one is identified with the other. In many oral communities, older people especially will say they cannot become Christians because they cannot read (see also Klem 1982, 37).

All books are sacred. In many oral communities the initial experiences of printed or written materials have been almost exclusively with the Christian Scriptures or associated religious materials like hymnbooks. Consequently any subsequent printed materials they receive are treated with similar reverence and awe and often regarded as having magical properties.

Literacy means wealth. Besides the economic advantages that education can bring to an oral community, many also perceive that literacy skills are a powerful means of communication with the supernatural, especially ancestor spirits, and can persuade them to release wealth and power to those so skilled. "Cargo cults" in Papua New Guinea are an example of this. In some places this sort of perception has meant a large initial enrolment of people in literacy classes, but a sharp falling off when no wealth appears as a result of their efforts.

Reading is meaningless sound-calling. In some cases people learn to match sounds with symbols without perceiving that any communication of meaning is involved in the process. This is especially so when learning a trade or national language but can also happen with people's own vernacular. The result is simply sound-calling, often done at a rapid rate, in a ritual type of performance. This is intended to bring prestige and status to the reader, but not necessarily intended to communicate anything meaningful to anyone.

PRESSURES EXPERIENCED BY ORAL COMMUNICATORS TO BECOME LITERATE

The heart cry of many contemporary educators in developing countries, like Paulo Freire and Frank Laubach, and the graphic message of novels like *Nectar in a Sieve* (Markandaya 1982), is that poverty, ignorance, and oppression are directly related to illiteracy. While there is some truth in this, it is not the whole story by a long way, but it is still widely accepted as a valid claim by both literates and oral communicators in the areas where these conditions prevail. As a result the following pressures are brought to bear on oral societies.

Economic Pressures

Many individual families believe that in order to survive economically in the present, and to have security for the future, their children must be formally educated so that they can obtain paid employment. This will often require the children to leave home and complete secondary and higher education in an urban situation. Adults too will undertake literacy programs in the belief that they will be able to obtain a paid position either in their rural location or by leaving their family and working for extended periods in a city. Oral communities will encourage literacy programs in their midst in the hope that this will in some way bring economic prosperity, perhaps through cooperative trading companies or other similar ventures. Pressures of this kind can motivate people to become literate, but it may be a very limited kind of literacy, restricted solely to economic needs, and if economic rewards are not forthcoming, it can lead to disillusionment and rejection of literacy as a viable and relevant skill.

Political Pressures

The past fifty years have seen a great turmoil of political activity in most developing countries. People have emerged from colonialism and experienced much confusion as various political groups, both indigenous and expatriate, have sought to establish their particular political system as the dominant one. Many oral communities and individuals feel very ignorant and susceptible to exploitation because of their lack of formal education, and particularly their inability to read and write. Many believe that the only way for them to gain freedom from the particular oppressive system they are under is to become literate. Others feel motivated to become literate in order to be able to read and understand the different political ideologies and become directly involved in their activities.

Social Pressures

Many oral communities, particularly minority groups, have a very low perception of their status in society, which is largely determined by the fact that they are not literate, especially in the national language or prestigious foreign language that is used in their area. So the community and individuals feel very strong pressures to establish schools in their villages in order that some of their people at least may become literate and they as a group will become socially accepted and have greater status in the wider context of their society.

Religious Pressures

Although Christianity is not the only religion to apply this pressure, Christian missions are certainly very zealous about making their converts literate. The explanation for this zeal is usually that it is necessary for the converts to be able to read the word of God for themselves and so progress to Christian maturity. However, for many churches and missions, literacy and church membership are very closely linked, and as indicated above in the matter of perception of literacy, many people identify one with the other, and so the matter of literacy becomes not simply a matter of progress but of spiritual salvation. Whatever the perception, Christians in oral societies often feel they are only second-class Christians if they are not literate.

These are some of the pressures brought to bear on oral communicators in order that they might become literate; the issue is not literacy for the sake of literacy alone. If we are considering literacy, we need to be very aware of these pressures and their effects on oral people.

Pressure of Literacy Reversion

Another pressure to be considered is the one that is just the reverse of those above, the pressure to revert to nonliteracy. Even where people have had a number of years of formal schooling, if they return to an oral community where literacy skills are not used on a regular basis, there is a strong possibility that they will lose those skills. Klem observes,

> If there are 70 percent non-readers in an area you cannot expect illiteracy to decline. But if the non-readers are a minority of 35 percent or less, illiteracy could be expected to decline [Nasution 1972, 7]. [Nasution] therefore considers that for a community to reach the take off point for modern industrialization at least 65 percent of the population must engage in reading. Then the primary school graduates will be supported in their use of reading skills and reversion can cease to be a threat. . . .

> Many students who learn Christianity in the schools return to non-reading, non-Christian communities and proceed to give up both literacy and the forms of Christianity dependent upon it. (1982, 14–15, 39)

These pressures are very real and, as indicated, can have a profound effect on oral communicators. So if literacy is an option that we intend to use in communicating the Christian message to an oral society, we must be aware of the pressures at work in that society and determine that our use of it will not affect oral learners in the wrong way.

NONLITERATES BECOMING LITERATE: THE PROCESS INVOLVED

Chapters 5–7 indicated the worldview characteristics, communication skills, and principles involved in communicating to oral, event-oriented people.

All of the issues discussed there are of vital importance when considering the matter of nonliterates becoming literate. It is not necessary to repeat the details of those issues, but it is helpful to consider again some of the main points mentioned there.

Worldview. Oral communicators have a different worldview from literates. An oral person's worldview is based on sound and the interpretation of auditory messages. The literate person's worldview is based on sight and the interpretation of visual symbols and messages.

The way people think. Oral communicators usually think in a concrete, relational way or an intuitional way, or a combination of these. The literate person, on the other hand, is a conceptual thinker. What this amounts to is that for an oral communicator to become truly literate involves a lot more than simply acquiring a new skill. It also involves worldview change and changes in thinking processes. An oral communicator may acquire literacy skills and learn to read fluently, but when it comes to comprehending the information, there may be many misconceptions and misinterpretations, simply because that person is still an oral communicator. The key to our understanding of this matter is that oral communicators process information differently from literates. We must keep this in mind in any proposal to bring literacy to an oral community that we might consider.

THE VALUE OF LITERACY TO AN ORAL SOCIETY

We have indicated above the kinds of pressure that are brought to bear on an oral society in today's world. These pressures often convince many of those societies that literacy and formal education are to be achieved at all costs. We may fear the bad effects of people yielding to these pressures without good support and guidance, but we must also concede that literacy can bring many benefits to oral societies.

Economic Value

Once people become literate, the possibilities for economic progress increase dramatically. In rural areas especially the opportunity for developing small businesses and cooperatives is greatly enhanced if some of the community at least is able to read and write. There is also much less likelihood of people being cheated and deceived by unscrupulous traders when those traders realize that they are dealing with a significant number of literate people.

Political Value

In the political ferment that is very much a part of life in most developing countries, oral communicators, especially in minority groups, can feel quite marginalized and unsure of what role they have to play in these events. This is basically because they are not familiar with the information and knowledge about the new political ideologies and proposals that are current in their area. Even if only a small percentage of their community are literate, they can explain these political matters to the wider community, who can then have some confidence about participating in the political affairs of their society and making a worthwhile contribution to the debate on relevant issues.

Social Value

We may question the motives of people who want to become literate purely to achieve higher social status. However, we must consider the context of many of these oral societies, especially the minority groups. These groups are often very susceptible to oppression and exploitation by larger power groups, and this situation is made worse if the oral societies have a low esteem of themselves and feel helpless to do anything other than accept the treatment given to them. If literacy in either their own vernacular or a national language can help to raise their self-esteem and give them confidence in their own society, then it will certainly be a value worth considering.

Educational Value

Oral communicators will usually not perceive this value quickly, as they regard the education that they have received orally as being of primary importance. Apart from the economic, political, and social advantages indicated above, the education they would receive through literacy is usually regarded as foreign and irrelevant. If this literacy program is in the national language or an international language such as English or French, and if it is carefully related to the learner's own context, then it should be of value to the individual and the community. Being exposed to the vast amount of information available in the new language should mean that the learner's life will be enriched, and through that person, the whole community. However, that will depend a lot on the literacy program.

Spiritual Value

Oral communicators are usually very aware of the supernatural and are interested to learn what Christians teach about this, but they might not see literacy as an appropriate way for them to do so. However, once they have chosen to follow Christ, there is a much greater motivation for them to want to know God's word, and this can be a key for developing a literacy program among them. To gain the greatest value from such a program, it would need to be accompanied by vernacular Scripture translation.

THE IMPORTANCE OF VERNACULAR SCRIPTURE TRANSLATION

The issue of vernacular Scripture translation has been a contentious one almost since the time Scriptures first came to be written. In the time of Christ, the Jewish authorities would not permit the Hebrew Scriptures to be translated and written in the local language of Aramaic, even though oral translations were made in Aramaic in the synagogues each Sabbath.

> In the synagogues the scriptures were read in Hebrew and then translated into Aramaic, for the majority of the people (and virtually all the women) were . . . Am-ha-ares . . . who could neither read nor correctly understand the Hebrew. (Moore 1946, 321)

The reader held the Hebrew scroll, but the translator was not allowed to have any written Aramaic notes of any kind. He was required to give an oral paraphrase that correctly expressed the meaning of the text, because it was held that a word-for-word translation would mislead the people (Klem 1982, 63).

In the medieval church the Latin Vulgate was considered by the church hierarchy to be the only translation that should be used. Men like Wycliffe and Tyndale faced intense difficulties and persecution as they sought to prepare a translation in the common English language. Both history and modern linguistic research have proved that vernacular translation and presentation of Scripture is the most effective way to bring God's word to any people.

God . . . uses the language and thought patterns of those to whom
He speaks. . . . He moves into the cultural and linguistic water in
which we are immersed in order to make contact with us. (C. Kraft
1979a, 10–11)

The language of the heart is difficult to stamp out. It is learned from
the mother's lips and spoken in the house. It is an inner sanctuary
where the outside world cannot penetrate. It is jealously guarded
because it enhances a sense of peoplehood. . . . The language aspect
of social structure is specially important because the Good News
of God's acts must be told in words. Missionaries who skillfully use
social structure at this point are intelligent stewards of God's grace.
(McGavran 1980, 218–20)

Some of the reasons that vernacular translation and presentation of
Scripture is so effective are as follows:

Clear understanding. When people hear a message in their own mother
tongue, there is much less chance of misunderstanding the true meaning of
that message. This is particularly true when we are talking about a message
such as that of the Christian Scriptures. This contains a wide range of concepts
and experiences, and if these are new concepts and experiences for the
person concerned, then it is going to be especially difficult for that person
to understand them clearly unless they are explained in their own language.
Hearing the message in a trade language or some other language will usually
mean that some of the terminology is incorrectly or only partially understood.

The language in which a message is given has a powerful effect on
how it is heard. It must be one for which the hearers can understand
all aspects of the topic being presented. Because the Christian
message deals with conscience and personal feelings, the clearest
understanding comes in the language of the home and daily life.
(Dye 1985, 103)

Acceptance. A person's own language is much more than a medium of
communication. It is an integral part of their whole cultural context. Therefore
when a message is received by people in that language, it is more likely that
they will respond positively and feel that the message is something that
"belongs" to them. A message received in another language usually carries
with it connotations of "foreignness" and perhaps oppression.

> Almost without exception, missionaries will be well advised to learn the language of their respondent culture. . . . If one wants to communicate Christ to a people, he must know them. The key to that knowledge always has been, and always will be, language. (Hesselgrave 1978, 250)

> Even where the national language is understood, it may carry a paramessage such as "This message is not for you unless you change your cultural identity." Usually where this paramessage is present, the style of church service, the particular sins in focus and other aspects of the message follow the national culture, and thus reinforce the idea that conversion and culture change are synonymous. (Dye 1985, 103)

Relevance. A message received in a person's vernacular speaks to their heart in ways that no other language can and makes the person feel that the message is relevant to their needs. Another language will not speak with the same incisiveness or power and will more likely give the impression that it is intended for someone else.

All of the above reasons help us to understand that the spiritual value of a carefully implemented vernacular literacy program, linked to Scripture translation, can be the greatest value of all to any oral society.

IMPLEMENTING A LITERACY PROGRAM

In considering a strategy for implementing a vernacular literacy program, we are not so much concerned as to whether we feel the program will be valuable to the people, but whether we can make it appropriate, relevant, and interesting so that the people themselves will perceive it as a valuable asset for them individually and for their community.

A Program that Is Appropriate

One of the most important things to keep in mind is the need to maintain a balance between the use of cultural oral skills and fulfilling the felt needs of the people to achieve certain goals through the attainment of literacy skills. The people must be able to see literacy as a gain without feeling that they are suffering loss of something valuable to them and undergoing major changes that they may later regret. In other words, an appropriate program is one where people are becoming literate without losing orality!

This would mean that oral communication forms are not ignored or put aside but utilized in a literacy program. In this way the communicational impact of those forms would not be lost, and the people's cultural identity and skills would be preserved. Guidelines for developing such a program are suggested by Susan Malone for the Umbungu people of Papua New Guinea and would seem to be appropriate for other language groups also:

1. The authority structure will follow those traditionally used in the clans; in larger areas, it will follow those used by the government.
2. The structure of the education program will implement traditional learning styles but will also utilize new styles of communication and teaching where appropriate.
3. The program will exist and expand only upon the acceptance and good will of the local people. Both the receiving group and the source group will have major responsibilities towards the program, and if one part fails in their responsibility, the work will cease among that group.
4. The program will be structured in such a way that the self esteem of the learners and their positive attitudes towards their culture and language will be enhanced. (1985, 13–14)

Malone has also prepared other helpful and more detailed outlines for the implementation of such a program (1987b, 10–11, 19–23; 1989, 5–15). Her emphasis, as indicated above, is that the program must be one that "fits"—fits the people's culture, fits the total context of the people's needs and aspirations, and fits the requirements for maintaining an ongoing relevance to the people and their community.

Paulo Freire in both *Education for Critical Consciousness* and *Pedagogy of the Oppressed* emphasises that education is not for the purpose of adapting people and pressing them into a predetermined mould. Rather it is to promote dignity and integrity, and to make people aware that they have the power to create their own culture and mould their own history. In bringing the word of God to people, we would want to go further and bring them into a right relationship with God, through Jesus Christ, which will enrich their whole personality and change their eternal destiny. But it is important for us to keep in mind what Freire is saying: that in implementing a program such as vernacular literacy we are not simply imposing a foreign system of communication upon people, which may produce results valuable only to those introducing the program. Freire also emphasises the importance of dialogue with students and the need to treat adult students as equals (1973, 46–48). These, of course, are important characteristics of oral communication.

Oral communicators will usually perceive literacy and printed literature as noncultural and "foreign," whether they regard it as desirable or not. Christian communicators working amongst oral people, who make it their top priority to distribute printed literature and promote literacy, will also be classified by them in the same way. Therefore it is important for such communicators to take an interest in and make use of the oral communication skills of those people.

CONCLUSION

For oral communicators the issue of literacy can be a very complex one. Their natural response may be to reject it as foreign and irrelevant, but the pressures of the situation in which they live may force them to regard it as a priority goal in life. This could lead to them leaving their own home and locality and having their whole lifestyle transformed. Christian cross-cultural communicators who may be considering implementing a literacy program in an oral community must therefore be careful about how that is done, and the following guidelines are suggested in the approach that should be taken:

Be thorough. Especially in initial research, so that there is a clear understanding of the complexities involved in the situation and what options are available for program development.

Be sensitive. Understand what the people's needs and aspirations are. What are their fears and weaknesses? What are their communication skills? Remember that it needs to be a receptor-oriented program. For oral communities, the printed or written word must be heard, and it must be recognised as their own.

Be patient. Finding the most effective literacy program will not come easily or quickly. Be prepared to change and revise. Be prepared for disappointments and setbacks. Be an encourager to those who embark on the program with you. Be prepared to wait for the right time and conditions. Jacques Ellul makes some very relevant and stimulating comments about the written and the spoken word: "The written word is just a mummy whose wrappings must be removed someday—not to discover a few bones, but to breathe life into it again" (1985, 47). That needs to be our goal also, that in bringing literacy to oral communicators we bring words that breathe life.

It is important at this point to remember that our aim in this chapter was not to consider how we can introduce literacy to an oral society, but rather what is the place of literacy in an oral society. We have considered a number of issues relating to literacy and oral communicators and the possibility of implementing a literacy program among them. It is possible now for us to sum up some important conclusions about this. In planning a communication strategy to oral people, whether for preliminary evangelism, leadership training, or any other program, the following are important matters for us to remember:

Literacy should not be a top priority—unless special circumstances demand it. Our top priority is effective communication of the word of God. As we have already discussed in detail, this is not dependent at all on literacy. Literacy can be an important and relevant part of the strategy, but it needs to be developed carefully. It should not be presented as an inevitable process, nor made to appear as if it is much superior to oral forms of communication and learning. Jesus did not use literacy, although the option to do so was open to him, yet the fact that he carried out an effective communication program cannot be denied.

Literacy should not be a substitute for any of the oral learning skills of the society, nor should it have the effect of diminishing the value of oral skills. It would be tragic if oral communicators, with their prodigious memories and other oral skills that have such potential for the learning and teaching of Scripture, should have those skills eroded. We would not want them to finish up like so many Western Christians who, although they have sung certain hymns many hundreds of times, still cannot remember the words unless they have a book in front of them!

Literacy is very difficult for many to achieve. As we have discussed above, it is not simply a matter of learning to relate sounds and words to symbols. It involves a completely new cognitive process and eventually leads to a major worldview shift. Therefore it is important to ascertain carefully just what percentage of the community needs to become literate in order to achieve the particular literacy-oriented goals that the community may have, so that unnecessary burdens may not be placed on the community either for the learning or teaching of literacy.

Literacy is a valuable tool. It can be the means of tremendous benefits, spiritually and in many other ways, for both individuals and for communities. Among oral people, where they perceive literacy to be desirable, our aim should be to implement a literacy program that is appropriate and will see people becoming literate without losing their orality.

9

DEVELOPING AN EFFECTIVE COMMUNICATION PLAN FOR MINISTRY TO ORAL COMMUNICATORS

INTRODUCTION

This plan is a number of things:

1. It is a way of describing how we will go about reaching our goal or solving our problem.
2. It is a way of thinking about the future, so that we will make the right decisions about the different ways our plan can go ahead. For the Christian communicator it is a process of making sure our plans will be what God wants. This will mean study of the Scriptures, prayer, and ongoing research.
3. Its development demands goal setting, which makes it possible to measure how well our plan is progressing.
4. It is based on receptor-oriented communication theory.

Good communication planning is essentially a good understanding of the audience, an adaptation of the message, a measuring of effectiveness, and an analysis of the results (taken from Søgaard 1988). The purpose of this chapter is to bring together the research findings, communication principles, and evidence from the Bible and use them to put together a general plan to bring the Christian message clearly to oral people. This general plan can then be applied by Christian communicators in their specific situation for evangelism, Bible teaching, or leadership training.

In seeking to develop a good communication plan for oral people, we will use the circular planning model of Dayton and Fraser (1980, 32) as our basic framework (see fig. 13 below). This has the following features:

a. It presents a comprehensive approach to Christian cross-cultural communication. This means it can be applied to evangelism, Bible teaching, and Christian leadership training.
b. It is adaptable to the culture of the missionary and the culture of the people.
c. It applies management principles to the missionary task.
d. Being a circular model, it does not follow direct, linear thinking.
e. Its emphasis is on people rather than methods.

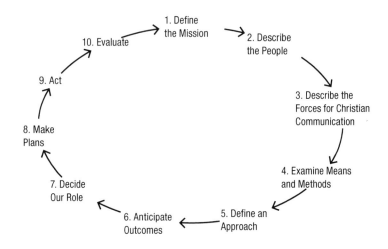

Fig. 13. Dayton/Fraser planning model
(adapted from Dayton and Fraser 1980, 32)

1. DEFINE THE MISSION

Defining the mission means to indicate what the primary purpose of this communication plan will be. In this case we want to design a plan that will be useful to those who are ministering to oral communicators around the world. When we talk about ministering to people, we are referring to the following:

a. Making oral communicators aware of Jesus Christ, how he can meet their particular needs, and all that they need to know in order that they may understand the reality of his salvation in their lives.
b. Communicating to them what will help them to become established in their faith and in their local church.
c. Communicating to them what will lead them on to maturity in Christ so that they in turn can minister to others, particularly others who are oral communicators like themselves. This aspect of ministering will include programs to develop indigenous Christian leadership.

2. DESCRIBE THE PEOPLE

One of the most vital aspects of communication theory is that if communication is going to be effective, then it must be receptor oriented, which means that the communicator must have a thorough knowledge of his or her audience; in this case, oral communicators. It is also significant to note that, although this particular group of people is scattered all over the world, they share a number of characteristics that are very important for us to know about if we are going to be able to develop an effective communications strategy among them. We need to understand as much as we can about oral communicators and in particular their worldview. The characteristics of oral communicators have been considered in chapters 1 and 2, and although they are broad in scope, they provide useful guidelines for our research into the particular oral community with which we are concerned.

Although the information given in chapters 5 and 6 may seem a somewhat detailed treatment of the audience that we can expect to encounter in attempting to communicate to oral societies, it is only just a hint of the amount of audience research that will need to be done if communication to an oral society is going to be effective. Not only do cross-cultural workers need to understand the particular needs of oral communicators, but each group must be dealt with in terms of its uniqueness. This means understanding their language, social structure, political context, and economic situation.

We need to ask questions like the following:

- How does group orientation express itself among these people?
- What values does it promote and how are these taught?
- Is there a particular focus for their time concept?
- Are there particular events or ancestral heroes that have a special significance for them?
- What features are evident in their culture that show they are concrete relational thinkers—myths? Parables? Proverbs?

Perhaps they are intuitional thinkers. Whatever they are, we need to know, and we need to know how these thinking processes are exhibited in this particular group. The people must be understood in terms of their total cultural context. This will mean careful and thorough observation on the part of the communicator. Every aspect of their life and experience needs to be noted and analysed, especially rituals, processions, and other activities connected with religion and beliefs in the supernatural. Communication forms must also be noted and classified as to whether or not they are suitable for presentation of the Christian message.

Decision-making processes are, of course, a very significant part of the people's experience, and in our presentation of the Christian message we are calling upon people to make decisions that will totally reshape their lives. Therefore the communicator needs to know how these oral people make the really important decisions in their lives, what are the cultural factors that influence this, and who are the decision makers and/or opinion leaders in the group.

The most effective communication will take place when the communicator and the receptor are participating in the same frame of reference as the oral society. This is also the best way for the communicator to gain an understanding of the group's own felt needs and where the people are in relation to their awareness and understanding of the Christian message. This is likely to be much more accurate than attempting to judge it from a cultural distance or from reports of other people. The diagrams in chapter 5 can be used to help the communicator's understanding of this important issue.

By doing all of the above we can build up a comprehensive picture of the characteristics of the people with whom we are working and how well they are prepared to receive the Christian message. The communication principles as set out in chapter 5 must be very much to the fore of our thinking and planning at this stage.

Oral Communication Skills

The communication skills of a people are a very important part of their description. The skills are described in some detail in chapter 2, but there will be many others that are not listed there. The communicator will need to look for the skills that are used by the receptor group and observe them carefully. It is important to note the ways in which those skills may be unique to that group. For example, as mentioned previously, storytelling is common to all cultures, but most cultures have their own unique ways of presenting these stories. The communicator will need to discover these things and determine what will be the most appropriate forms to use for the presentation of the Christian message. In most cases it will probably not be appropriate for stories to be told by people from outside the cultural group. It will also need to be seen how these skills are used for teaching and remembering cultural values.

Biblical Models

Biblical models, as described in the section on scriptural precedents, will not provide any direct information for the purpose of describing the people under consideration. However, it is important to note any areas of similarity between the cultural context and characteristics of the receptors and those of the people of the Scriptures. These can then be used in subsequent stages of the plan.

Case Studies

These are described in chapter 6, and although they do not provide direct information for the purpose of describing the receptor group, they can be used in the same way as the biblical models. That is, the communicator should note carefully any areas of similarity between the cultural context and characteristics of the receptors and those of the case study groups. In particular, communication forms that are similar should be highlighted.

The forms used in a successful plan in another oral group could provide guidelines to a suitable plan for the receptor group.

By working through the above research framework, the communicator can build up a comprehensive description of the receptor group. It will focus on the fact that they are oral people, on their communication forms, and on how they can best receive the Christian message. This description of the people then becomes the basis for our communication plan.

3. DESCRIBE THE FORCES FOR CHRISTIAN COMMUNICATION

In this part of our plan we need to consider what resources, in terms of personnel and organisations, are available to us in order that we can achieve our original purpose. Our main supply of resources will come through the body of Christ—through local churches, cross-cultural missionaries, or parachurch organisations.

The Local Church

The people we are seeking to reach are located in people groups all over the world, but wherever they are, the ideal communicators are Christians who are part of the same people group. They will not have the problems of trying to overcome language and cultural barriers, and they will understand the needs of the people better than anyone else. However, they may need support from outside their own local church in the areas of finance—to be able to implement an effective plan—and training—to equip them with the particular skills and knowledge they need to carry out their plan.

Cross-cultural Missionaries

If the particular oral community we are seeking to reach has very few or no Christians, then the next most effective communicators will probably be Christians located in people groups adjacent to that community. Another possibility is to use expatriate missionaries who are willing and interested to work in that community. Either of these possibilities would involve Christians working as cross-cultural communicators, and they would need special training if their ministry were to be effective.

Parachurch Organisations

In parachurch organisations we are looking for resources that can help us particularly in ministry to oral communicators. This would include individuals or groups working in radio, television, video, and audiocassettes. Drama groups, singing groups, and other groups skilled in the use of cultural art forms can also be used very effectively. It would include groups such as Bible translators who could assist in general understanding of cultural and language factors, and could also be instrumental in preparing materials in the vernacular that could be used in the oral communication process.

Recruiting and Training

Because of the special skills involved in communicating to oral people, the personnel described above will need to undergo training in order that their contribution to the plan will be effective. Training required will vary, of course, depending on the resource group concerned, but even resource people from within the people group will need to be made aware of how they can use their own cultural forms in this process. Parachurch groups will need special consideration, as they may be committed to a Western approach and it may require long-term negotiation to persuade them to make the changes necessary for their contribution to become appropriate for the particular target group. If they are not prepared to do this, their particular resource may have to be bypassed. It is more important to have resources that are appropriate than to use an inappropriate one simply because it happens to be there.

Technological Resources

There may be some technological resources available that would be appropriate to use. These could include radio and television, and perhaps also mobile phones, which could be used in conjunction with radio for a "talk-back" presentation. Such resources would need to be carefully researched to determine whether they would be useful in the oral communication plan (see appendix A).

4. EXAMINE MEANS AND METHODS

This is a vital area of the strategy, as we try to assess just how the job will be done. Choosing the right means and methods can make a very significant difference to the end results. As has been described in chapters 3 and 4, people like Jesus and Jeremiah used oral means and methods of communication to present the word of God to the oral communities in which they lived, and they did so with dramatic effect and response.

In *Strategies for Church Growth*, Peter Wagner gives some useful guidelines when faced with apparently "resistant" groups of people and points out what we have just mentioned above, that communication methods and a thorough understanding of a group's worldview are vitally important.

> One of the dangers in using the resistance-receptivity axis is that you can come to the conclusion that a given people group is resistant to the Gospel because they haven't responded when as a matter of fact, they have been receptive all along, but you have been using the wrong methods for reaching them. . . .

> Sometimes communication is at fault. The message is not getting through.

> Missionaries worked for 25 years with the Tiv tribe in Central Nigeria and saw only 25 baptized believers as a result. Their medium of communication was preaching, which they had learned in Bible school was the way to evangelize. A few years ago some young Tiv Christians set the Gospel story to musical chants, the native medium of communication. Almost immediately the Gospel began to spread like wildfire, and soon a quarter-million Tiv were worshipping Jesus. The Tiv were not as resistant as the missionaries thought. A change in method brought abundant fruit. (1987, 91–92)

On the other hand, it would not be right for us to think that choosing the right means and methods is all that there is to it. We are still dependent on the Holy Spirit to produce worthwhile and abiding results, and we must look to him to guide us in the methods we choose and to work through those methods to make them effective.

Some thoughts from Dayton and Fraser will be helpful to guide us as we consider appropriate means and methods:

> More and more we are inserting technology between us and those we seek to evangelize. Our contacts are increasingly more impersonal and fleeting. Yet all our studies indicate that the nature and length of contact is the single most important element in evangelism.

> Methodology that is ill conceived and applied without regard for the culture and context of a people leaves us with no humanly justifiable reason for believing that anything is happening that will further the evangelization of a people.

> The multiplicity of peoples we face requires a multiplicity of methods. Every method excludes some types of people from authentic witness and must be complemented by other methods that include them.

> There is something contradictory about trying to create an indigenous church by using nonindigenous methods. (1980, 259–60)

For Western-oriented communicators the temptation is to promote "hi-tech" methods. These are the things that excite us and communicate effectively to us. But for oral communicators the methods that appeal to them must include people to whom they can relate, and must involve their own personal participation.

In choosing means and methods we need to keep in mind what was stated above in "Describe the People"; that is, what are the characteristics of oral communicators in general, and then what are the unique features of the particular people group we are attempting to reach? With these things in mind we can establish certain principles of communication that will guide us as we choose the appropriate means and methods. Some of those principles would be:

a. The communication should be oral and event-oriented.
b. Culturally appropriate communication forms should be used.

c. The means and methods used should be such that the people contacted should be able to carry on the communication without having to rely on substantial support from outside their group.

These principles are the basis for the following, which will be a key factor in determining the effectiveness of our means and methods.

Use an Appropriate Delivery System

Consider carefully the ways in which material can be presented to oral communicators. Look for culturally appropriate communication forms. This does not mean that all cultural communication forms can be used. For a number of reasons, some forms may be quite unsuitable. Others may need to be adapted or changed somewhat. The key in this matter is patience and sensitivity. Whoever is preparing the material will need to be in close consultation with the people concerned and alert to negative responses to new techniques that may be tried; not that a new technique should be completely discarded because of a negative response, but it does need to be known and evaluated.

Keep in mind that for oral people, a presentation is not usually a one-way exercise. Performance and participation are central in their concept of appropriate communication. Dialogue and group discussion should be used to make sure that people have a chance to participate and become involved in the presentation. We will now consider some of the communication forms that may be present in an oral society and which could be appropriate to use as means and methods in the communication strategy being worked out for the specific group of oral communicators.

Graphic and Plastic Arts
This would refer to drawings, paintings, carvings, and sculptures. Each cultural group's artwork needs to be considered in terms of its own individual cultural context. In many cases the artwork of a culture is associated with religious ritual and traditions, and so caution must be exercised to ensure that unwanted traditional religious concepts are not communicated when attempting to use those art forms to teach Christian truths. Sandgraphs in Angola and iconographs among the Australian Aborigines (see ch. 2) are examples of very effective use of cultural art forms for evangelism and Christian teaching.

In many cases the artwork may be linked with a story, song, or proverb, both as a memory aid and to add cultural distinctiveness. So if there are indigenous Christian artists in the receptor group, encourage them to become an active part of the group's ministry of Christian communication (see also "The Use of Visuals with Oral Communicators," appendix B).

Singing

Every oral society has its own traditional songs, which are a very important part of its culture. For oral cultures, singing is not simply for entertainment, nor are the songs only for special occasions, but rather, singing is an integral part of the whole social structure.

Some of the songs are used to recount traditional myths, legends, and moral codes. It is quite possible that these forms could be adapted for use with Bible stories and Christian teaching. Scripture memorization by means of traditional chants or songs is also a real possibility. We have many examples of this in the Scriptures themselves (see ch. 4). Some of the case studies mentioned in chapter 6 are also graphic examples of how well this medium works. Klem's experiment with this medium in West Africa appears quite dramatic from a Western viewpoint. There he asked a local group of Christians to set the first six chapters of the book of Hebrews to their own music and to practise it so that it could be recorded on cassette. By the time they were ready to do this—a matter of a few weeks—not only had the whole church memorized these Scriptures but most of the local townspeople as well! (See Klem 1982, 167–78.) Who wouldn't like to see this rate of Scripture memorization in their local church and community?

As we can see from the above examples, vernacular Christian songs can be very popular with the whole community and may have a wide scope of ministry. The indigenous system of singing can be used for praise, worship, thanksgiving, teaching, evangelism, and Scripture memorization.

Drama and Dance

Drama and dance are very much a part of an oral society's way of expressing their feelings as well as communicating traditional stories and rituals. These art forms were also an integral part of ancient Jewish culture and are mentioned numerous times in the Scriptures as a way that the Israelites expressed their faith and communicated their teaching about God.

Unfortunately, contemporary Western evangelical Christianity does not on the whole approve of these art forms, and as a result evangelical missions do not encourage them among converts. Also, in many areas dancing is in bad repute with Christian churches because of previous immoral practices. However, drama and dance can be used very effectively in the presentation of Bible stories and contemporary Christian parables. The Christian corroborees performed in Central Australia are a good example of this (see ch. 6). In a similar cultural context, in the Torres Strait Islands, the local people dramatized many of the Bible stories, and these were produced on video. The videos were then distributed around the islands, where video sets were readily available, and they were received with great interest and enthusiasm (Kennedy 1983).

Drama and dance are marvellous ways for oral communities to show participation, identification, and response, and thus demonstrate their own cultural characteristics. Therefore they must be given serious consideration by Christian communicators, as they are a very dynamic form of communication.

Storytelling

There are many cultural variations of storytelling, and in most cases it would be classified as an art form. It is important to realize that many cultural forms of storytelling are completely different from the Western cultural style, and simply putting a vernacular translation of a Bible story into a Western storytelling format does not mean that it will communicate as effectively as their own cultural stories do. The communicational form must be culturally authentic and relevant. Remember too the oral culture's characteristic of perceiving the spoken word as having special power. It is a living word, from a living person, and the who, when, where, and how of storytelling are likely to have great significance. Everybody loves a good story, but making it a "good" story for a specific receptor group may take extensive research and patient perseverence with a variety of techniques and formats that are suitable for that receptor group.

The storytelling of Jesus was unique. It was obviously culturally acceptable and relevant, but it was more than that. His storytelling was a considerable cut above that of any other storyteller in that context, and hundreds of people would flock to hear him, hour after hour, day after day; "No one ever spoke the way this man does," they said (John 7:46). These same stories are now known around the world, probably more so than any other stories in history.

They have proved to be highly adaptive to different cultural contexts, and especially to oral people.

Where there are Christian leaders who have this storytelling skill, they especially should be encouraged to make good use of it in the ministry of Christian teaching. This is the sort of art form that lends itself to use with media such as audiocassettes, radio, and video.

Poetry

As has been indicated previously, poetry is a significant form of communication in many oral cultures. In some Middle Eastern cultures at this present time, any important message to be communicated to the people is usually prepared in poetic form. Some years ago, it was most interesting to hear a news report about a top-level conference of the PLO (Palestinian Liberation Organisation) in North Africa. A key person at the conference was a nationally recognised poet. During the conference a new manifesto was drawn up for the PLO. The poet's job was to put the manifesto into poetic form, and then it was circulated to PLO groups throughout the Middle East and probably around the world. There it could be sung, chanted, or recited until it was memorized. Compare the communicational effectiveness of such a means with that of a similar political statement produced in a Western, literacy-oriented society and distributed as a printed document, say, by saturation mail-out. The majority of recipients would at best briefly scan the document before discarding it. But even if it were retained and carefully read, its contents would probably not be remembered for more than a few days.

So if poetry is a feature of an oral society, then it can be a tremendous asset for presenting the Christian message to that society. It can also be used in training Christians in Scripture memory, catechism learning, and other aspects of Christian knowledge that will lead them on to spiritual maturity. Christians within such a society will need to be recruited and encouraged to prepare Bible stories, catechisms, and other Scripture teaching material in their own poetic format.

The thing is, do we really grasp the potential of these indigenous oral means and methods for our communicaton plan? Or do we feel they are always somewhat less effective than the literacy-oriented ones with which we ourselves are familiar? If we hesitate and procrastinate in this area of our communication plan, it is very doubtful that we will produce a program that is either dynamic or effective.

Using Modern Technology

Modern technology should also be considered; for example, audiocassettes, radio, video, and audiovisuals. However, the communication principles relevant to an oral culture, as discussed above, need to be firmly kept in mind.

Cassettes, for instance, can be a marvellous teaching tool that fits in remarkably well with an oral communication system. But if the message on the cassette is a bare, monologue reading, poorly presented by someone who is only just functionally literate, then it will not be recognised by the people as one of their cultural communication forms, even if it is in their own language, and the communicational impact will be very small (see appendix A).

Radio, because it is an aural medium, has great potential for communicating to oral people. However, the standard one-way, one-off presentation normally employed by radio studios severely limits the effectiveness of such communication. Within the last few decades, a phenomenon has transformed what were rather lacklustre radio programs in Western countries and introduced what could be a most effective program format for communicating to oral people. It is known as "talk-back" radio, whereby listeners can call the radio station by telephone and participate in the topical discussion, news comment, favourite song selection, or whatever type of program is using this format. Such a format is ideally suited to oral communicators, because it is an aural medium that also provides opportunity for participation. Its use is probably limited to an urban context where telephone facilities are available, but even so, it could still reach large numbers of oral communicators.

Video programs have great potential because of the opportunity for people to be involved in their own presentations. This can be done by means of drama, singing, artwork, storytelling, poetry, and any other appropriate forms of communication. The video medium combines visual and aural forms, but the strong attraction would be that the people themselves are participating and then viewing the program.

Visuals need special treatment if they are to be effective with oral people. Audiovisuals, picture books, comic books, flip charts, flash cards, and posters are just a few of the many visual presentations that are used among oral people. Many literacy-oriented people make the assumption that visual presentations of this kind are easily understood by people, even if they cannot read. We should never make that assumption. Appendix B outlines some of the difficulties that oral people encounter with visuals, and these must be kept very much in mind if we are planning to use visuals in our communication plan. Careful research and preparation are essential if a visual presentation is going to communicate clearly and accurately to oral people.

Therefore if modern technology is going to be used, the focus of presentations should be on aural rather than visual, although visuals when properly prepared can be a very useful supportive feature.

Research, Pretesting, and Evaluation

As with each stage of the planning cycle, research and evaluation are essential elements. However, during the "Means and Methods" stage it will probably require a considerable amount of time to be invested. After thorough research has been done, it is important to carry out pretesting of a particular method, on a small scale, just to ensure that it is going to achieve the response that was anticipated. Making a few adjustments prior to embarking on a major communication project is much to be preferred to the disappointment and expense involved in trying to patch up something that is found to have numerous mistakes and shortcomings.

Ongoing evaluation and adjustment of means and methods will be necessary in order to ensure that the communication remains relevant and dynamic. As people progress through the understanding and awareness stages of Christianity, their needs in this area will change. Dayton and Fraser's comments are helpful at this point:

> There are several additional questions that we need to ask before we choose a method. Does the method(s) take them through a process so that they are moved closer to a decision for Christ? Does it attempt to challenge them for commitment too soon? Does it respect the common patterns by which they deliberate about major decisions that affect religious allegiance? Does it utilize their social structure in terms of decision-making patterns that require the cooperation or consensus of certain individuals? (1980, 289–90)

Means and methods are part of the communication strategy that will require a great deal of time and effort, but this will be amply repaid in knowing that the communication attempted will be the most effective possible.

5. DEFINE AN APPROACH

We have come to a stage where an appreciable amount of research has been done on the people we are attempting to reach; what resources, in terms of personnel and organisations, would be available for use in this project; and what means and methods would be most appropriate for them to use. We have now reached the stage in the process where we need to make definite decisions about what we are going to include in our plan and what we are going to leave out. In other words, we need to make an outline of our plan. This statement does not need to include a lot of finer details, but should be a strong outline of how we perceive the project is going to be accomplished.

The preliminary statement should include a short-term plan, an intermediate plan, and a long-term plan, so that people can understand the process we expect to be working through. It should also include details of our relationships with existing churches (if any), other Christian agencies, and our own supporters. It will spell out the purpose, objectives, and goals of our plan. The statement could be prepared in a form such as the following:

- We intend to evangelize the _____ group of oral people. (Instead of "evangelize" we could substitute "give basic Christian teaching to" or "provide a leadership training program for.")
- We will begin with the _____ group, which is located at _____. This group is at _____ on the Engel/Søgaard scale.
- Our short-term plan will be to _____. (This could be to make an initial contact or to establish good relationships with the local church.)
- We will do this using the following methods: _____, which will be carried out by these people: _____.
- Our intermediate plan will be to _____. (This could describe how oral communication techniques will be used to bring people to a level of knowledge of the gospel and to see a church planted amongst nonliterates, or describe how a local church will use oral communication to increase the knowledge of their own members and become an effective witness in their oral community.)
- We will do this using the following methods: _____, which will be carried out by these people: _____.

- Our long-term plan will be to see that ___ percent of this group will move from ___ to ___ on the Engel/Søgaard scale. We anticipate that this will take the following time:
- Phase 1. _____
- Phase 2. _____
- Phase 3. _____
- We will share our plan with _____ (people, churches, mission agencies, supporters) and ask them if they can assist us in the following ways: _____.

Having made this preliminary statement, we are now in a position to review all that has been done to date. It helps us to see not only what we plan to do, but what our approach is going to exclude. That is, we will not need _____ (e.g., literature, radio, and TV programs); we can avoid _____ (certain difficulties and problems). It also means we can ask ourselves some relevant questions to determine whether we are still on track with our original purpose and whether it is valid for us to assume that we can achieve that purpose. This means questioning the assumptions we have about ourselves, the people, churches, and groups we are planning to work with, the people we are endeavouring to reach, and the context in which our communication will take place. Having done that, we may need to restate our plan, but then we will be ready to move ahead with the next step.

A case study of a World Vision project carried out in India gives us some idea of what can happen at this stage of the plan:

The Perathur Community Development Project was started in October 1985. The target area consists of four villages with a population of about 5000 people. The Christian population in the target villages is very small except in one village. The project was initiated by the Church of South India which has three C.S.I. churches and a hospital situated in a radius of 10 km. The concern of the church was to help the villagers, who are mainly Harijan being exploited by the high caste Naidus.

The project initiated the following programmes in October 1985:

1. Liberate them from the clutches of the high caste.
2. Educate them to demand their rights from the Government.

3. Free them from the bondage of ignorance especially from superstitious belief.
4. Develop them socio-economically by providing skills training and economic assistance.
5. Provide non formal education to the adult illiterates and formal education to the children.
6. Provide them the much needed medical facilities.
7. Communicate the Love of Christ and disciple them.

Our main objective in running this program was to communicate the Gospel meaningfully and disciple them. The diocese appointed an evangelist, who visits the four villages. Besides this the 8 project staff were also involved in presenting the Gospel. But the reaction of the community to the message was one of indifference. The community was suspicious of our motives.

The following questions are asked frequently:

1. Do you want to convert us by providing monetary benefits?
2. Do you want to make money by highlighting our plight to others?
3. Are you really interested in our welfare?

The project staff's efforts to answer these questions did not bear fruit because the community people were indifferent and cold to our programmes. There were not any interesting programmes through which our conviction and motive of involvement could be explained. Our study and research showed that the reason for misunderstanding our motives is mainly lack of communication. Hence we decided to use pre-recorded cassettes to address the needs of the people and present Christ. (Joseph 1987)

This brief glimpse into a case study helps us to realize the difficulties that may be encountered. It also underlines a basic premise of any realistic mission strategy: that although a group of enthusiastic, dedicated Christian people initiate a program that is well planned and is based on sound objectives that will provide practical, social, and spiritual benefits for all people in the target area, it does not mean that they, or their program, will be accepted, welcomed, or understood by the people concerned. Effective communication will only be achieved as the principles in chapter 5 are followed through. We will continue to follow this case study as we move through the stages of our strategy.

6. ANTICIPATE OUTCOMES

It is important that we look ahead and anticipate what the possible outcomes of our strategy could be. This is not only concerned with avoiding problems that may occur, but also with making the necessary provision for the positive, successful response that could happen. If our strategy indicates that we will achieve certain results over a specified period of time, then we need to be ready at that time to deal with those results. For instance, if our strategy was to encourage the people to use some of their own music to go alongside Scripture texts and some basic Christian materials, and they became enthusiastic about this, then we would need to have ready a graded set of translated evangelistic and Bible teaching materials so they could move into those while their enthusiasm and excitement were still strong.

While not being necessarily pessimistic, we must be prepared for negative as well as positive responses. Means and methods that work with one group may not work at all with another, even though they seem to be very similar. We need to anticipate such possibilities and be ready with alternatives that can be brought into the plan at short notice. We must also be prepared for changes, too: changes in the people we minister to, changes in the churches and organisations with whom we are working, and possible changes in communication technology. As we consider these anticipated outcomes, they need to be fed back into our plan and so keep it relevant and effective for our situation.

7. DECIDE OUR ROLE

As we are part of the communication plan, we need to give due consideration to the role we will have in that plan. We must be able to make an accurate assessment of our capabilities and spiritual gifts and decide what role will best accomplish the strategy we are pursuing.

There are at least two aspects of our role that will need to be considered. Firstly, our role in relation to our colleagues who are working with us on the project: we could be an administrator, facilitator, or instructor, or something similar. Secondly, our role in relation to the people we are contacting: we may assign ourselves a role for this, such as Bible translator, or agricultural advisor, but the group itself will also assign a role to us, and it will be important for us to discover what that role is. It could be a low status role, such as foreigner or source of material goods only, which would mean that our influence on the group or its individuals would be very minimal. We should try to achieve some sort of significant status role, such as advisor, teacher, or friend, which will allow us to have some positive influence.

The important thing to remember about our roles in the group is that our main purpose is to bring about change. This will probably involve changes in ourselves, our organisation, and our plan, but primarily we are looking to see significant changes in the group that will move them along the awareness-knowledge-conversion-incorporation path that is projected in our plan. The Dayton/Fraser "Axioms for the Change Agent" are worth noting as helpful guidelines for us in this step. They are:

- Look for needs.
- Take a long range view.
- Take your time.
- Involve as many people as possible.
- Be open to new ideas.
- Break it down into steps.
- Use examples.
- Build on success.
- Affirm progress.
- Uncover the future slowly.
- Expect to be led by the Holy Spirit. (1980, 425–28)

If we can keep these in mind, then our roles are likely to be a meaningful and effective part of the overall plan.

8. MAKE PLANS

We should now be in a position to follow up on our preliminary plan by describing our goals and making the plans we feel will be necessary to achieve those goals. We will need to make a definite choice of the means and methods we will use at the beginning. We need to decide on the people who are going to be involved, what training and preparation they will need, and what facilities and equipment will be required. We also need to calculate the resources that will be needed and how finances, cooperation, and prayer support can be raised.

Our plans could look something like this:

Long-term goal: 7–8 yrs. Thirty percent of the _____ group will move from ___ to ___ on the Engel/Søgaard scale.

Appoint people to be responsible for monitoring and reporting progress of this goal to those directly involved in the project and to those supporting by prayer and other means.

Short-term goals: 1–2 yrs. Preliminary research. Establish contact. Two missionary families to locate amongst the people. One local family (pastor, evangelist), one expatriate family (communication and technical skills). Learn language. Determine priority needs of group.

Appoint people to these positions and provide them with a detailed job description that will include a time frame for them to aim at achieving their goals.

3–4 yrs. Construct suitable recording and programming facilities. Prepare programs in the local language to meet some of the priority needs. Use indigenous music and storytelling techniques. Use cassettes or other contemporary aural devices (CDs, MP3 players, etc.) to contact people in surrounding districts.

Decide who will construct studio facilities and arrange contract with them. Appoint people needed to produce the programs (e.g., scriptwriter, recording technician, musicians, dramatic readers, and actors).

Because of the very nature of the variety of communication methods and their effectiveness, it would not be appropriate to set goals beyond this stage. A lot will depend on the initial research, contact with the people themselves, and their response to the missionaries who come to live amongst them. Local drama may be the most effective way of communicating new ideas, and so on. However, it is important to have these definite goals and plans clearly before us so that the next stage can be embarked upon with confidence.

9. ACT

We now come to the stage in our plan where we begin to put into action the research and planning that we have done to date. Unfortunately, in many mission communication plans, this section takes up a large percentage of the effort of those involved. But if we want our communication to be effective, then adequate time must be given to the research and planning stages, then when it comes time to put it into practice, the "action" part will flow with a minimum of holdups, problems, and misunderstandings.

We have just talked about setting goals, researching means and methods, and gathering resources, but for the action stage this procedure is reversed. First of all we gather together the resources we have planned to use, then we start to apply the means and methods we have selected, then we evaluate our progress to see if we are achieving our goals.

Gathering Resources

Depending on the plans we have made for communicating to a particular nonliterate group, this will mean selecting the personnel we need, ensuring that they receive the necessary training, and putting them into position with the necessary equipment and support that they require. For instance, if we are planning to use cassettes as part of our communication program, we will need to provide recording and programming equipment, as well as tapes and players to use in distribution of the completed programs. Funds for this may be available through church and mission agencies, but it may require a special fundraising project to ensure that these resources are available when they are needed.

Applying Means and Methods

The means and methods decided upon in the planning stage are now put into practice. In each case, research concerning those means and methods needs to be done. It is important that we take adequate time to carry out the necessary research and not skimp on this at all, even if there are many pressures to "get on with the task." If we have allowed two years for people to do language learning, to research the communication system of the group, and to establish good contacts and rapport, then we need to be patient during that time, supporting the project with prayer and allowing more time for this research to be completed if necessary.

Baptist missionaries working in Central Australia with the Aboriginal people spent about ten years just encouraging the small group of Christians in the community, learning the language and culture of the people, and eventually convincing them that it would be a positive and acceptable thing to use their own cultural communication forms to express their Christian faith and teach the Christian message. This led to a thriving church that was really excited about the gospel and eagerly communicating it to others.

Applying the means and methods also needs to be done in partnership with the people themselves. They need to be involved in, and if possible directing, the way the communication forms are introduced and used in the oral community.

The case study from India, introduced above, provides us with an example of how a communication plan can be implemented, in spite of initial setbacks:

> The project staff spent a considerable amount of time in researching the communication needs and issues of the people. To identify the needs and issues we asked the following questions:
>
> 1. Who is my audience?
> 2. Where are they?
> 3. What are their needs?
> 4. How best can I meet their needs?
>
> We identified the problems of the community in the following spheres:
>
> 1. Education
> 2. Health
> 3. Social Evils
> 4. Family Life
> 5. Life in the Community
>
> After identifying the needs, a thorough research was done on the people's knowledge, attitude, belief and behaviour in relation to each of the issues. After the research, cassette programmes were produced on the following topics:

Way to Progress	Evils of Drinking
One God One Community	Unity and Involvement
Hope in Christ	Health and Hygiene
Eternal Life	Forgiveness

> The issues were dramatized and the Gospel teaching was interwoven into each cassette. A sincere attempt was made to present the Gospel on all the cassettes. (Joseph 1987)

This is a good example of how to apply the communication principles outlined in chapter 5 to this situation. The Christian group concerned did not panic or become depressed by the initial rejection and indifference of the people. They simply went to work with the thorough research and personal involvement that was needed to produce an effective communication program. Not indicated in the brief summary above is the fact that the group used puppets and street theatre, as well as the cassettes, in communicating to the areas of need identified by their research. These presentations were followed up by close personal contact with the people, so that they came to realize that the mission team was genuinely interested in them as people. The result was a much more positive response.

Reaching Goals

Having established goals at our planning stage, we need to keep those clearly in mind, and not be content simply with having some good activity going, even if it is proving to be acceptable and enjoyable by all concerned. We need to ask ourselves, "Are we achieving our goals?" "Why or why not?" "Are our goals realistic?" "Is our time frame realistic?" and so on. Then, in the light of our answers to these questions, we need to determine what replanning we need to do and whether there needs to be any correction to our program—which means we are already into the final stage of our plan: evaluation!

10. EVALUATE

Although evaluation is placed here at the end of the cycle, as we have indicated previously, it is a constant part of the planning process. When we evaluate the various stages in the communication plan, it is important to keep in mind that we are evaluating performance and effectiveness and not persons. We need to ask the questions as outlined above in stage 9 to evaluate our *goals*. We need to evaluate our *means and methods*.

A missionary in the Philippines knew that cassettes would be effective in communicating the Scriptures to the oral community in which he worked, but he tried six different program formats before he found one that really communicated. But once he found and developed that format, the ministry of the gospel in that area was transformed. Previous problems of motivation, cooperation, and distribution of the materials just disappeared (see Benn 1980–87; also the case study titled "The Philippines: Singing, Dialogue, Questions" in ch. 6).

We need to evaluate our *resources*. Have we estimated our needs correctly? Are there new or different resources that we need? Has the project been a good stewardship of resources? Finally, we have to evaluate *personal performance*. This is not, as we have mentioned, an evaluation of a person, but of the work they have done. This will need to be done in relation to the job description prepared for each person and according to the standards and time frame established beforehand with the personnel concerned.

The case study from India indicates the positive impact of the plan on the target communities:

Impact of the Cassettes

1. They have imparted information on various issues to the people.
2. They have educated the people about their privileges and rights.
3. Motivated them to act upon this information.
4. Provided entertainment.
5. Strengthened their cultural values.
6. Made people come together to become involved in the development process.
7. Made the church become actively involved in the ministry.
8. The message of the gospel was made meaningful to them.
9. Youth associations were formed.
10. New believers were added to the church.
11. The attitude of the people changed.

The following activities were initiated/conducted:

1. Cottage prayer meeting.
2. Sunday School and Vacation Bible School.
3. Children's retreat.
4. Youth retreat.
5. Women's retreat.
6. Special meeting.

As a result of the cassettes, the community has moved from negative attitude to positive attitude towards the Lord Jesus Christ. The questions raised by the community were answered and the doubts removed. (Joseph 1987)

Limitations of space do not permit a full report on the effectiveness of all the communication forms used in the above project. Suffice it to say that the effect was truly remarkable. The cassettes in particular had dramatic and far-reaching effects, so much so that in the areas of need that were targeted, traditional deep-seated attitudes and prejudices within the community were significantly changed. In one instance the provincial government actually reversed previous legislation in order to ban the distribution and sale of alcohol in the community. Youth associations and other community groups were formed to tackle some of the problems highlighted on the cassettes. Health/hygiene advice as well as warnings about alcohol abuse attracted keen attention and brought a positive response. Project staff and local church workers such as the evangelist were welcomed and urged to visit homes throughout the villages. Correct understanding of the message and messengers brought about a complete transformation of response from the community.

CONCLUSION

Case studies like the above help to reinforce the basic thrust of this book: that the message of the gospel of Jesus Christ is applicable to all people and all needs everywhere, but that it must be communicated effectively before people can respond to it. In using the term "effective communication" I am referring to communication that achieves the desired results. Such communication is not produced from a plan that is put together in about ten minutes! It comes from a plan that is based on extensive research and planning. It is one that includes all the communication principles as set out in chapter 5.

The plan presented in this chapter may seem to be rather detailed, but this is simply because it reflects the communication principles and research of the previous chapters, upon which it is based. Achieving effective communication to oral people can be a complex matter. If this is going to be attempted by Western, literacy-oriented personnel, then the research and planning must be thorough and extensive and the whole approach carefully integrated.

Commenting on the World Vision project in India, Viggo Søgaard made the following statement:

> We should understand that projects will only reach their goals and potentials if good and integrated holistic communication is taking place. The cassette is one of the effective tools available to us, but the crucial point is the staff members themselves, and the working out of an integrated communication strategy. This is not a task to be taken lightly. Careful training and planning must take place. Then for the glory of God, men and women will be reached with the true Gospel of Jesus Christ. (1987, 6)

"Not a task to be taken lightly" is a key phrase that underlines all that is involved in an effective communication plan. It means thorough and careful research, patient testing and evaluation, along with a genuine concern for and involvement and identification with the receptor group. Developing an effective communication plan for ministry to oral people can be summed up in the following way:

1. Know the people—their worldview, especially their oral characteristics, their total context, and their felt needs.

2. Know how they communicate—their oral skills and communication forms, their significance in the cultural context, and their appropriateness for use with the Christian message.

3. Know our message—this must go beyond standard clichés and religious formulas. Our message must be clear and meaningful, appropriate and applicable to the people's context and felt needs.

This information should be carefully integrated as a proposed plan and implemented in true humility and dependence upon the Holy Spirit. Then we can expect the resultant communication to be effective and the results to bring honour and praise to our God.

CONCLUSION

Throughout the course of this book we have discussed and affirmed a number of proposals related to oral, event-oriented people and the communications system that is part of an oral society. These proposals are as follows:

1. The great majority of people in the world today are oral communicators. This number includes many who have received some kind of literacy training or formal education, but who prefer to be oral communicators and so have not maintained their literacy skills. In spite of the extensive literacy programs as well as the formal and informal education systems around the world, the number of oral communicators is steadily increasing. The highest percentage of oral communicators is in the developing countries of the world, which also have the highest percentage of people who have yet to receive a clear presentation of the Christian message.

2. The oral communication system has the same capacity as the system of literacy for receiving and transmitting the Christian message, and oral people are just as capable as literacy-oriented communicators of receiving and understanding all that they need to know about Christian teaching. The way that they achieve this is quite different from the way that literates would do it, as they use different ways of thinking and different learning skills, but it is certainly not inferior.

3. The precedents of Scripture—in particular, Jesus' messages in the Gospels and the original presentation of the Old Testament Scriptures—show that these messages were all prepared for oral communicators and presented to

those people by means of oral communicational forms. Thus these precedents of Scripture are excellent models for anyone who is considering development of a strategy for communicating God's word to an oral community.

4. The main proposal presented in this book is that where people are members of an oral, event-oriented society, or where this is still the primary orientation of the society, then the oral, event-oriented communication techniques that are part of that people's own culture are the most appropriate ones to use in the communication of Christian truths to those people. This is not to say that they are the only communication techniques that could be used—there may be a number of reasons for supplementing them with other communication techniques—but they will be the most appropriate and also the most effective as far as achieving meaningful, relevant communication. These oral, event-oriented communication techniques are also the most appropriate for training oral communicators to become Christian leaders in their society.

OTHER THEMES OF THIS BOOK

While the above proposals form the basis for the development of the message of this book, there are some features that become prominent and which could be described as its major themes. These are as follows:

The identity of oral communicators. Who exactly the oral communicators of the world are, and what their communicational skills are, is discussed in detail in chapters 1 and 2. This information helps us to identify the oral communicators who are present in a multiplicity of contexts around the world today. Identifying them, and recognising their uniqueness in terms of worldview and thinking processes, means that we can have a solid foundation for building a plan of effective communication to them.

Principles of communication applicable to oral societies. Communication theory, applied specifically to oral societies, is developed in chapter 5 and examples of its successful application are described in chapter 6. This is a major thrust of the book, to show that regular principles of communication can be applied to a group of people as broad in scope as the oral societies of the world, and successful results can be predicted with reasonable confidence.

Effective strategies developed for communication to oral societies. Chapter 6 describes some case studies of effective strategies that have been developed for communicating to oral societies. These were mainly in the area of initial evangelism to a group, but in some cases the same strategy was adapted to encompass more advanced Christian teaching. Chapter 7 shows how an effective plan can be developed for the vital ministry of training Christian leaders in an oral society, and chapter 8 discusses the relevant issue of literacy in an oral society and how an effective plan can be developed to meet that need.

Thus it can be seen that the development of effective communication plans for ministry to oral societies is a major point of the book, and this culminates in the outline of such a plan in chapter 9.

A POSTSCRIPT ON THE BOOK TITLE

The title *Don't Throw the Book at Them* may seem a little strange or provocative. The purpose of the title is to act as a stimulus to the thinking of Western people who are or may become involved as cross-cultural communicators to oral, event-oriented people. The people in that category have, for the most part, been through a Western formal education system of learning and been raised in a literacy-oriented society. So even though they may study cross-cultural communication and understand its principles, their basic assumptions and worldview will still be literacy-oriented. However, if these people are evangelical Christians, then they have come to believe in Jesus Christ as the Son of God, and they regard everything that he said and did as not only extremely important but also unquestionably correct.

So when faced with the challenge and opportunity of bringing the Christian message to an oral community, the normal reaction of these people may be, "We must teach at least some of these people to read and write, and then give them the printed word of God in their own language," or "We should try widespread distribution of tracts and Scripture portions among these people—some of them must be able to read, and they can explain it to the others." My hope is that the title of this book will cause people to stop and think and to consider that there are other, more relevant possibilities for communicating effectively to oral people, and that Jesus himself is the prime example. The option for Jesus to use literacy and literature, and to write his own book, was certainly there. He was literate himself, as were a number of his disciples. But he deliberately chose to use the oral communication system that all of the people knew and used rather than the literacy-oriented system that was limited to a small, elite group. If that was the way that Jesus chose, then if we are involved in a similar situation with regard to an oral society, we would certainly be foolish not to give it our serious consideration. Many situations will not be similar, of course, but in relating to an oral society, wherever that may be, there are going to be many elements of commonality, and this makes it imperative that we understand clearly the principles and techniques used by the master communicator himself and see how they would apply to the situation concerned.

THE MESSAGE FOR MISSION WORK TODAY

The important message is the fact that the major part of cross-cultural mission activity today is being carried on in areas that have a high percentage of oral communicators. The areas of the world that are still waiting to receive the message of Christianity for the first time have an even larger proportion of oral people.

Over the last twenty years or so mission interest has focused on what is known as the 10/40 Window, an area of the earth that extends from North Africa across South Asia, between ten degrees north to forty degrees north of the equator. This area contains, among other things, the vast majority of the unevangelized people of the world, and Christians have been challenged to focus their efforts on this area in order to bring about world evangelization as soon as possible. It is important to note that this area also contains a large majority of oral communicators.

Unfortunately, in many of these areas it is still the standard practice of the missions or national churches to use Western, literacy-oriented methods of communication for both evangelistic and leadership training aspects of their mission program. The main message of this book is that there are other, better options that can be used—the same sort of options that Jesus used. In the light of the vast and increasing opportunities for evangelism available in the world today, it would be a tragedy if we failed to make the most effective use of these opportunities. By this I mean that we might fail to learn from the enormous amount of research into mission activity that has been carried out over the past thirty or forty years, particularly in the area of Christian cross-cultural communication. Oral communicators do not particularly need Western, literacy-oriented methods of communication either to hear the Christian message or to be built up and grow in the Christian faith. They need oral methods of communication that are appropriate to their own cultural context.

The information contained in this study can enable people to prepare an effective communications plan for ministry of God's word to an oral society. This study shows how it can be done; it also has case studies to show that it *has* been done before, in many parts of the world. The challenge is that it might be done soon for the many hundreds of oral, event-oriented people groups for whom the word of God has still to become a reality.

APPENDIX A

THE USE OF AUDIO EQUIPMENT AND CASSETTES IN ORAL SOCIETIES

INTRODUCTION

Our contemporary world has seen an incredible spread of cell phones, so that an almost unbelievable percentage of the world's population—possibly 80 percent—either own or have access to one. Because these are primarily audio devices, they are absolutely ideal for communicating to oral societies. Therefore they present a wonderful opportunity for Christian communicators to present the Christian message to oral people. To make effective use of these devices, Christian communicators would need to consider the following: What types of mobile devices are available in their area? Are they primarily audio devices, or do they have video capability as well? What is the most effective and economical way of presenting the Christian message through these devices?[3]

As seen in some of the case studies described above, audiocassettes can be a very effective tool in the overall program of ministering the Christian message to oral people. There are many examples of mission- and church-related audiocassette programs that have commenced with plenty of vision and enthusiasm, but which have just faded out and disappeared before very

---

3   Global Recordings Network (GRN) has produced some excellent training resources for those using mobile audio devices in their strategy; visit http://globalrecordings.net for articles and other tools.

long. The following segment is presented as an aid and guideline for those who may be considering establishing a cassette ministry or are already involved in one. Following these guidelines, and adapting them to the context of the oral community concerned, should help people to avoid the pitfalls that are there and to develop a program that will convey a relevant and dynamic message to that community.

The other important consideration is the availability of cassette players, which are no longer being manufactured in the quantities they were previously. Therefore, with many other mobile audio devices available, thorough research must be done to see what will be the most effective type of program or whether a number of devices can be used effectively.

ADVANTAGES OF AUDIOCASSETTES

1. *A mechanical method of oral communication.* The audiocassette is the extension of a person talking through a machine. In other words, it is a mechanical method of using the oral system of communication. Nonliterates are able to look past the technical apparatus and recognize the method of communication as one with which they are familiar, and therefore they have little problem in identifying with it.

2. *Matches traditional learning patterns.* Basically, the traditional method of learning is oral transmission and memorization. The audiocassette employs the same principle. The tape can be played over and over again, fifty times or one hundred times, so that the listeners learn the message by heart. The message will always stay the same.

3. *Availability and mobility.* Provided the cassette player is operating correctly, it can be used at any time of the day or night that is convenient to the listener. Players are available in battery-operated and hand-wind models, which means they can be taken anywhere at all. They are small and light, and not a burden for the pastor or evangelist to carry with them on their visitation program. The cassette tape too is small and compact. Many hours of messages and songs can be carried in a pocket. This provides the absolute maximum in terms of communicational availability.

4. *Ease of operation.* In spite of being a sophisticated piece of technical equipment, most cassette players are relatively easy to operate, and a few periods of instruction are all that is usually necessary for a nonliterate person to learn the required skills.

5. *Attracts attention and interest.* One of the amazing things about the cassette is the way it is able to attract and hold people's attention. It has been used in a remarkable way to break through many of the cultural, linguistic, and religious barriers that exist in the world today.

6. *Support to Christian witness.* The cassette can also be a great encouragement to Christians to become involved in witnessing. The cassette presents the message clearly and without faults or stumbling speech. As a new Christian uses the cassette, he or she learns more about the gospel and gains confidence in passing it on to others.

7. *Audience-specific.* Cassettes can be tailor-made to suit a specific audience. Unlike radio, they do not need to be programmed for a wide, inclusive audience. Local colour can be included through the presentation of local music and sound effects. They can be produced in the local language and dialect of the people. They can also be produced to meet specific needs of a particular audience and so be highly relevant to the listener.

8. *Dramatized soundtrack.* Cassettes can be produced with a dramatized message, songs, etc., to be used in conjunction with a mimed drama or puppet show, or with an audiovisual presentation using posters, pictures, or slides.

SOME DISADVANTAGES

1. *Impersonal.* The greatest disadvantage is the fact that a cassette is an impersonal device. There is no way that it can enter into a "life involvement" situation with the listener. No matter how clear or relevant the message may be, the listener needs to observe how the message is lived out in a person's life and how he himself can identify with such a person. The cassette message needs to be backed up by the testimony of a victorious Christian life, lived out in the listener's own context.

2. *Need for maintenance and repair.* All cassette equipment, no matter how expensive or how well made, will need regular maintenance and repair. The more the equipment is used, the more this need will be evident. Any church or mission involved in a cassette ministry must consider this aspect carefully, or the whole program could become ineffective. Personnel need to be assigned specifically to this task, to be given specialised training if needed, and also to be able to train others in basic maintenance procedures.

3. *The cost factor.* In some situations, the cost factor is a disadvantage that limits the usefulness of the cassettes. Where import duties are high and

living standards low, even basic cassette equipment can be very expensive, and a wide circulation of the cassette medium among nonliterates is not a practical economic proposition. In some cases, cassette programs can be subsidised by churches or missions from more affluent countries, but this is not without its problems, and it needs to be considered carefully.

It is important for the Christian communicator to consider that there are certain disadvantages with the cassette medium, but with careful planning and preparation these can usually be overcome. Because of the tremendous advantages in using cassettes, especially with nonliterates, the effort is certainly worthwhile.

PREPARING AN EFFECTIVE PROGRAM FOR USE WITH CASSETTES OR AUDIO EQUIPMENT

Audience Orientation

The audience is our primary concern. We need to understand their needs.

- We must provide answers to the questions they are asking and give teaching on the issues that are important to them.
- We must make the word of God relevant to them.
- We must lead them on to a deeper knowledge of Christ.
- We need to understand their perception. This means understanding their culture and worldview.
- We must present the message in a form that listeners can recognize as their own and that speaks clearly and dynamically to them.
- We need to look for their response and participation.
- The message needs to be prepared so that the audience can respond in a way that is culturally appropriate and meaningful to them.

The following four key questions are an excellent guideline to help establish a suitable audience orientation for producing effective programs:

1. Who is my listener?
2. Where is my listener?

3. What needs does my listener have?
4. How can I meet the needs of my listener? (Søgaard 1988)

Possible Program Formats

Program content can be considered in the following general categories:

1. Scripture text alone.
2. Presentations based on Scripture.
3. Presentations based on non-Scripture topics and themes (e.g., health and nutrition, agricultural development).

In category 1, the formats are somewhat limited because of the inflexibility of the text. However, the following formats could be used:

a. *Monologue.* This is the easiest to produce but has the great disadvantage that it can become very monotonous. Also, it may not be a culturally appropriate form of presentation. If monologue is used, it must be spoken well, with natural, oral style, so that the meaning is clear.

b. *Dramatization.* This will depend a lot on the translation, but where direct speech is used, a multivoiced production can be made, which adds reality to the presentation.

c. *Use of cultural forms.* This could include singing, chanting, a special storytelling style, or a combination of these. If the Scripture text can be prepared in this way, it will have a dynamic impact on the people, as they will recognize the form and be open to respond to it.

In category 2, presentations based on Scripture, the formats are unlimited but need to be based on the research that has been done to determine the needs, perception, and response of the audience. We can then choose a Bible story or series of Scriptures and base our message(s) on those. In this way we try to make an application of the Scripture to a culturally perceived need. Some possible formats are:

    d. *Monologue.* (See above.)

    e. *Dialogue*—topical discussions. This can be a most interesting way of dealing with topical issues. Two people discuss the issue, with one person asking leading questions and the other providing the Christian teaching on the issue.

    f. *Audience response.* This is basically a question-and-answer approach. The concept is to get the audience directly involved in responding to the teaching on the cassette. The format would be something like the following:

        i. *Introduction*: Explanation of program procedure.

        ii. *Message*: Could be a passage of Scripture, monologue story, dialogue, or fully dramatized presentation. Singing could also be used in this segment.

        iii. *Questions*: Questions are asked on the tape relating to the message. The cassette is stopped after each question so that discussion and Bible study can be carried on with the audience.

        iv. *Answers*: When the discussion and audience response is completed, the cassette is turned on again and the correct answers are heard on the tape. These could be Scripture verses, direct statements, or in the form of a song.

        The use of this type of format implies that a suitably qualified person will operate the cassette player and lead the discussion on the questions.

    e. *Testimonies.* Used in conjunction with a Scripture passage or a dramatized Bible story, a personal testimony can be a very effective message. It shows the reality of the transformation of people's lives through the power of Christ and the practical outworking of scriptural principles in people's everyday experiences.

    f. *Dramatization.* The aural message medium lends itself very well to the dramatization of a message. It is suited to a format which exploits a variety of voices and the use of sound effects. Not all Bible text is suitable for dramatization. But action and narrative passages, with a good amount of dialogue (or potential dialogue), can be presented very effectively this way. It is also possible to dramatize cultural stories and other nonbiblical stories and use them in conjunction with a Scripture passage or in teaching scriptural principles.

    In category 3, the formats used could be similar to those outlined for category 2. The program content would need to be determined by research into audience needs, but would deal with topics such as those addressed in a typical World Vision project in India, which included some of the following:

Evils of Drinking	Loan Repayment
Youth Involvement	Hope in Christ
Eternal Life	Health and Hygiene
Backyard Garden	Salvation

For example, in Papua New Guinea the people have an enormous fear of evil spirits, so a script prepared by PNG missionaries that we used very extensively, and very effectively, was called "Don't Be Afraid." This was then followed by a series of messages entitled "Creation to Christ," which was prepared by Global Recordings Network and adapted to the PNG context.

Voices Used in Recording

The choice of voices is a critical factor in achieving success with a recording program. Voices must be clear and acceptable to the audience, able to speak naturally and so that they will be understood. Ideally we choose mother tongue speakers, people in good standing in their community who are able to read a prepared text well or able to memorize it piece by piece and speak it well.

Identification and authorisation of the voices used may also be a critical factor. In the presentation of oral material on a cassette, the audience may have some very definite questions about the people who are presenting the material, such as:

- Who is the speaker, and where does he or she come from?
- Why is he or she presenting this message?
- How does he or she know this information?
- What authority does he or she have to tell it?

People may not listen to the message until they have acceptable answers to these questions. So an audio message may need a preface, a statement of identification and authorisation at the beginning. This may include the speaker introducing himself or herself by name and place of origin; a brief explanation that he or she was appointed to do the recording by the local church or some other recognized body; and a brief explanation that the message comes from the Bible, which is the word of God and the basis of Christian life and faith.

Equipment and Maintenance

Recording equipment is changing and upgrading at a rapid rate. Global Recordings Network is a good group to contact about suitable equipment and its cost.

Audio equipment may be personal property or belong to a mission or church. Whatever the case, the best maintenance of the equipment is preventive maintenance. The four worst enemies of audio equipment are heat, moisture, dirt, and vibration. However, a few simple guidelines can help to keep the equipment in a good working condition for a long period of time:

1. When the equipment is not in use, keep it in an airtight container or wrap it in a clean cloth inside a dry plastic bag. This will minimize the effects of dust and moisture and also keep out the cockroaches.

2. Keep equipment and tapes away from excessive heat, such as a cooking fire or stove. Do not leave exposed to the sun or in a vehicle that will be sitting in the sun. Tapes especially will soon buckle and become useless.

3. When carrying equipment anywhere, make sure it is protected from vibration. In a vehicle, put it on a cushion or folded blanket rather than on the floor. Carry it in a backpack rather than strapped on the back of a bicycle or motorbike.

4. Teach users how to handle and take care of the equipment and tapes.

5. Where batteries are used in the equipment, they need to be monitored carefully. Batteries can corrode and cause serious damage to the equipment. Batteries should not be left in equipment if it is going to be stored for a period of time.

USING AUDIO EQUIPMENT FOR EVANGELISM AND BIBLE TEACHING

Preparation

People who carry out this type of ministry need to make thorough preparation before they do so. This will include choosing the right message; listening to the program beforehand; reading the Bible passages referred to and doing any other necessary research on the subject under discussion; preparing questions to ask, explanations to give, and discussion points; and checking the equipment before going.

Presentation

When the audio equipment is taken to a village or town,

- Decide a good time when people will be free to listen.
- Choose a good place where the audience will not be interrupted.
- Get the people to sit around in a circle, so that all can hear well and also have a part in the discussion.
- Play one program and then stop. Do not play the next program until the first has been talked about and understood. Use the prepared questions to start discussion. Ask for further questions.
- Try to get as many people as possible taking part in the discussion.

Testing, Evaluation, Monitoring

Testing is a multifaceted task. It is a process of constantly monitoring both the production process and the actual communication process. It is of utmost importance to know how a particular program, or series of programs, performs in relation to the objectives. The testing or evaluation procedures should be built into the planning of production and outreach. Scripts should be tested, test recordings should be made and evaluated, and the final product should be tested before release.

Self-critique. The first step is your own self-critique. It is not enough to be hard on yourself when writing and producing. Listen critically to the production and try to put yourself in the place of the intended listener. There may be several things you are not satisfied with. Maybe the natural flow of a dialogue needs improvement. Try to ask yourself the critical questions that will make you satisfied that the production will be effective in communicating to the intended audience.

Internal evaluation. The next step is internal evaluation by your own colleagues and staff. For this purpose it is helpful to have an evaluation form which people can fill out as they listen. Make a list of the various segments of the program and ask people to rate them on a five-point scale. After successful internal evaluation, the program should be tested among the intended audience.

Individual testing. It is suggested that the first test be done with one individual. As he or she listens to the tape, the researcher will watch for any outward signs that may give clues to how the person understands the material. The listening should be followed by a discussion of the material.

Group testing. The programs will often be used in small groups, and it is therefore important to pretest the program in such a group. The procedure suggested for testing with one person can be used. Watch for responses as they listen. Do they discuss the person presenting the message or do they discuss the content? Do they make funny remarks? Do they fall asleep? Do they start discussing a completely different subject? Do they walk away? Afterwards, ask them to discuss the message. See if they have any suggestions for change or improvement, and see if they are interested to hear more programs of that type.

Field testing. This means testing the programs in a limited geographical area but under normal conditions. Construct a questionnaire that will cover all aspects of the production and distribution. Interview as many people as possible who are involved in the field outreach, as well as a cross-section of the audience.

Monitoring. Keep continual records of program production and distribution. Many lessons will only be learned over a period of time. It is also advisable to keep records of comments received concerning individual programs. Use all opportunities to encourage and receive feedback. Be a good listener!

RESOURCES

The following is a list of resource groups and people that may be very helpful to you in your ministry to oral communicators. They all have audio material available in many different languages.

- Global Recordings Network
- United Bible Societies (please note their *Audio Scriptures Workshop Manual*)
- Audio Scripture Ministries
- Wycliffe Bible Translators
- The JESUS Film Project (available in over 1,100 languages)

- Campus Crusade for Christ International (Cru in the United States)
- Faith Comes By Hearing[4]

The important thing to remember about audio messages is that they are a tool. They can be a very effective tool, and a tremendous asset to Christian communicators, especially those in a cross-cultural context. However, if they are going to be truly effective, they must be backed up by people—people who are living a victorious Christian life and who can demonstrate the reality of the Christian message within the cultural context of the people who are receiving that message.

---

4   Contact details for the above groups can usually be obtained on the Internet. If this is difficult, contact GRN and they should be able to provide the information you need.

APPENDIX B

THE USE OF VISUALS WITH ORAL COMMUNICATORS

INTRODUCTION

Visuals require special treatment, and those involved in communicating to oral people should remember that visuals are much more impressive to literates than to nonliterates. As Elliston cautions,

> Many assume that people in developing countries, especially people who can not read, can readily understand pictures and other visual aids. Some would even go so far as to suggest mistakenly that visual aids provide some sort of an "Intercultural language" which is understood by all. To these people it would seem that pictures, posters and other visuals can communicate where the spoken language fails.

> Many nonliterate adults perceive the picture as the article or thing itself rather than an abstraction of something else. Another problem which must be overcome is that there are only two dimensions in a picture and people are normally accustomed to perceive visual images in three dimensions. The lack of the third dimension in a picture may be confusing at first until one learns to "read" the third dimension into the visual cues of the picture.

People have to learn to "read" pictures in order to perceive the intended message just as they have to learn to "read" other abstractions. (1988c, 1)

Between 1982 and 1987, I was involved, along with a number of other staff members of Global Recordings Network, in the production of a series of Bible picture books, which were to be used in conjunction with vernacular cassette recordings. A total of 192 pictures were prepared in all, but before this was done, an extensive survey was undertaken of prospective users. Visits were made to Papua New Guinea, Indonesia, India, and Africa, as well as doing surveys in Australia. People were very positive about wanting to use the visuals, but more importantly, we gained some very useful information about the sorts of difficulties that oral people have in using visuals. In preparing a strategy for communicating to oral people, it is important that we understand these difficulties and seek to minimize them.

DIFFICULTIES ENCOUNTERED IN USING VISUALS WITH ORAL COMMUNICATORS

Misperception of three-dimensional pictures. In general, it is best to avoid using three-dimensional pictures; that is, pictures where perspective is an important focus. For an oral viewer, the picture is seen as two-dimensional. Large figures and small figures are seen as just that, and not as something in the foreground and something further back. Therefore pictures should be constructed in such a way that the figures and objects are predominantly on the same spatial plane. For this same reason, backgrounds should be kept plain and uncluttered. Extra details that are not relevant or essential to the purpose of the picture are only confusing and difficult for oral people to "read."

Inability to discern subtle colour changes. For this reason bold colours are usually preferred. Subtle shadings and pastel colours do not have the same appeal, nor are they as easy for oral people to "read."

Difficulty in constructing the whole from parts. It is extremely difficult for an oral person to recognize a figure as a person if the picture is only showing the top half of that person. Oral people are not used to "filling in" the missing parts of people or boats or houses that have not been included in the picture. Therefore it is important that figures and objects should be kept whole, especially those that are in focus in the presentation.

Confusion with composite pictures. By "composite picture" I mean a presentation where there is more than one picture on a page, or a poster that contains a series of pictures. Oral people find it difficult to distinguish between the pictures, even if they are marked out with very clear boundaries. Reading from left to right or top to bottom is not intuitive, and so the general effect is one of confusion. Therefore, composite pictures should be avoided. If in a presentation, or in telling a story, it is intended to use a number of pictures (and there can be many good reasons for doing this), present the pictures one at a time and make sure each picture is clearly understood before proceeding to the next. Economy of space, printing costs, and the problems associated with carrying and handling large numbers of pictures are all very strong arguments for using composite pictures, but they really amount to nothing if the end result for the viewer is confusion.

Symbolism, cartoons, and photographs. Symbolism, cartoon-style figures, and similar techniques such as stick figures should be avoided unless this style of artwork is already known and recognized within the particular receptor group. For literacy-oriented people these presentations can be very attractive and may appear to be a dynamic form of communication for use with oral people. But for the same reasons that have been mentioned above, oral people can have great difficulty in "reading" this kind of pictorial representation, and the possibility of misperception and misunderstanding is great.

It is the same with photographs. Research carried out by Bruce Cook in Papua New Guinea indicates that, contrary to what many would expect, photographs do not rate highly when it comes to communicating to oral people. This is largely because of the complex background details that are usually part of a photograph and which oral viewers find difficult to differentiate from the foreground. Realistic line drawings with plain, uncomplicated backgrounds are the best option to use with oral communicators (see Cook 1981). However, even the most carefully prepared pictures will not necessarily be easy for oral viewers to comprehend. It is a skill that they will need to learn.

Having stated all of the above, it must be acknowledged that visuals can be an asset in communicating to oral people. They will not be as dynamic, nor as clear, communicationally, as they are to literate people. However, if they are carefully prepared, they can arouse keen interest and also be a good memory aid for the listener as well as the person presenting the story.

REFERENCES

Adams, Bruce. 1979. Buried treasure. *Africa Now* (June–August): 5–6.

Albright, W. F. 1965. *Yahweh and the gods of Canaan*. Winona Lake, IN: Eisenbrauns.

Baird, Joseph A. 1969. *Audience criticism and the historical Jesus*. Philadelphia: Westminster Press.

Barclay, William. 1959. *Educational ideals in the ancient world*. Grand Rapids: Baker Book House.

———. 1966. *The first three Gospels*. London: SCM Press.

———. 1975. *Introduction to the first three Gospels*, rev. ed. London: Baker Book House.

Barker, Glenn W., W. L. Lane, and J. R. Michaels. 1969. *The New Testament speaks*. New York: Harper & Row.

Bateson, Gregory. 1958 [1936]. *Naven*. Stanford: Stanford University Press.

Beals, Alan. 1967. *Culture in process*. New York: Holt, Rinehart & Winston.

Benn, Keith. 1980–87. Unpublished articles, scripts, and prayer letters.

Berlo, David R. 1960. *The process of communication*. New York: Holt, Rinehart & Winston.

Black, Matthew. 1967. *An Aramaic approach to the Gospels and Acts: With an appendix on the Son of Man*, 3rd ed. London: Oxford University Press / Clarendon Press.

Boag, Charles. 1991. The grammarian fights back. *The Bulletin* (November): 26–30. Sydney, Australia.

Box, Harry. 1982. Central issues in communicating the gospel in Melanesia: With special focus on Papua New Guinea. MA thesis, Fuller Theological Seminary.

Bruce, A. B. 1973. *The training of the Twelve*. Grand Rapids: Kregel.

Bruce, F. F. 1979. Transmission and translation of the Bible. In *Expositors Bible commentary*, vol. 1, ed. Frank E. Gaebelien. Grand Rapids: Zondervan.

Burney, Charles Fox. 1925. *The poetry of our Lord*. London: Oxford University Press / Clarendon Press.

Carothers, John Colin. 1959. Culture, psychiatry, and the written word. *Psychiatry* 22: 307–20.

Carpenter, Edmund, and Marshall McLuhan, eds. 1960. *Explorations in communication*. Boston: Beacon Press.

Clinton, J. Robert. 1984. *Leadership training models*. Altadena, CA: Barnabas Resources.

Condon, John C. Jr. 1975. *Semantics and communication*. New York: MacMillan.

Conn, Harvie M. 1984. *Eternal Word and changing worlds*. Grand Rapids: Acadamie Books.

———, and Samuel F. Rowen, eds. 1984. *Missions and theological education in world perspective*. Farmington, MI: Urbanus.

Cook, Bruce. 1981. *Understanding pictures in P.N.G.* Elgin, IL: David C. Cook.

Dalmann, Gustaf. 1929. *Jesus-Jeshua: Studies in the Gospels*. Trans. Paul Levertoff. London: SPCK.

Dayton, Edward R., and David A. Fraser. 1980. *Planning strategies for world evangelization*. Grand Rapids: Eerdmans.

Denoon, Donald, and Rod Lacey, eds. 1981. *Oral tradition in Melanesia*. Port Moresby: University of Papua New Guinea.

Disch, Robert, ed. 1973. *The future of literacy*. Englewood Cliffs, NJ: Prentice-Hall.

Dorson, Richard. 1972. *African folklore: Papers of the African Folklore Conference*. New York: Anchor.

Dye, T. Wayne. 1985. *The Bible translation strategy*. Dallas: Wycliffe Bible Translators.

Edersheim, Alfred. 1962–63. *The life and times of Jesus the Messiah*. 2 vols. Grand Rapids: Eerdmans.

Eisenstein, Elizabeth. 1979. *The printing press as an agent of change: Early communications and cultural transformations in early modern Europe*. 2 vols. New York: Cambridge University Press.

Elliot-Binns, Leonard. 1956. *Galilean Christianity*. Chicago: Alec R. Allenson.

Elliston, Edgar J. 1983. Maasai leadership development: An emerging process. *East Africa Journal of Evangelical Theology* 2, no. 2: 20–31.

———. 1988a. Developing nonliterate Christian leaders. Prepublication manuscript, Pasadena, CA.

———. 1988b. Home grown leaders. Unpublished manuscript, Fuller Theological Seminary, Pasadena, CA.

———. 1988c. Use of pictures with nonliterates. Unpublished manuscript, Fuller Theological Seminary, Pasadena, CA.

Ellul, Jacques. 1985. *The humiliation of the Word*. Grand Rapids: Eerdmans.

Engel, James F. 1979. *Contemporary Christian communication*. Nashville: Thomas Nelson.

Erickson, Edwin. 1985. Oral theology and dynamic Christianity. DMiss diss., Fuller Theological Seminary.

Eubank, Allan. 1989. Dance, drama and music in evangelism. In a report presented by the Christian Communications Institute at the Lausanne Congress on Evangelism, Manila, Philippines, June 1989.

Farrall, Lyndsay. 1981. Knowledge and its preservation in oral cultures. In *Oral tradition in Melanesia,* ed. Donald Denoon and Rod Lacey. Port Moresby: University of Papua New Guinea.

———. 1984. *Unwritten knowledge.* Victoria, Australia: Deakin UniversityPress.

Fernea, Elizabeth W., ed. 1985. *Women and the family in the Middle East.* Austin: University of Texas Press.

Finnegan, Ruth. 1970. *Oral literature in Africa.* London: Oxford University Press.

———, and Robin Horton, eds. 1973. *Modes of thought.* London: Faber & Faber.

Foster, George M. 1973. *Traditional societies and technological change.* New York: Harper & Row.

Freire, Paulo. 1972. *Pedagogy of the oppressed.* New York: Herder & Herder.

———. 1973. *Education for critical consciousness.* New York: Continuum.

Fuglesang, Andreas. 1973. *Applied communication in developing countries: Ideas and observations.* Uppsala, Sweden: Dag Hammarskjold Foundation.

Fugman, Gernot. 1969. Church growth and urbanization in Papua New Guinea. MA thesis, Fuller Theological Seminary.

Gerber, Virgil. 1980. *Discipling through theological education by extension.* Chicago: Moody Press.

Gerhardsson, Birger. 1961. *Memory and manuscript.* Copenhagen: Almquist & Wiksells.

Gibbs, Eddie. 1981a. *I believe in church growth.* Grand Rapids: Eerdmans.

———. 1981b. Shaping the church to fit the non-book culture. Unpublished manuscript, Fuller Theological Seminary, Pasadena, CA.

Goody, Jack, ed. 1968. *Literacy in traditional societies.* London: Cambridge University Press.

Gordis, Robert. 1971. *Poets, prophets and sages.* Bloomington: Indiana University Press.

Gould, Syd W. 1986. Missionary strategy and Scripture reception. MA thesis, Fuller Theological Seminary.

Hall, Edward T. 1959. *The silent language.* Garden City, NY: Doubleday.

———. 1983. *The dance of life.* Garden City, NY: Anchor.

Hesselgrave, David J. 1978. *Communicating Christ cross-culturally.* Grand Rapids: Zondervan.

Hian, Chua Wee. 1987. *The making of a leader.* Downer's Grove, IL: InterVarsity Press.

Holland, Fred. 1978. Theological education in context and change: The influence of leadership training and anthropology on ministry for church growth. DMiss diss., Fuller Theological Seminary.

Hollander, Edwin P. 1978. *Leadership dynamics.* New York: Free Press.

Horton, Robin. 1967. African traditional thought and Western science. *Africa* 36: 50–71; 37: 155–87.

Houston, Tom. 1978. *Communicating the good news in a television age.* London: British & Foreign Bible Society.

Hovey, Kevin G. 1978. New Life Forum: A description and communication analysis. Unpublished manuscript. Ambunti, Papua New Guinea.

———. 1980. Training non-literate church leaders. Unpublished manuscript, Fuller Theological Seminary, Pasadena, CA. In personal archives of C. H. Kraft.

———. 1986. *Before all else fails . . . read the instructions! A manual for cross-cultural Christians.* Brisbane: Harvest Publications.

Howat, Lois. 1974. The Talking Bible. *Missiology* 2: 439–53.

Hunter, Archibald. 1973. *The work and words of Jesus.* Philadelphia: Westminster Press.

Jeremias, Joachin. 1954. *The parables of Jesus.* Trans. S. H. Hooks. London: SCM.

———. 1969. *Jerusalem in the time of Jesus.* Trans. F. H. Care and C. Care. Philadelphia: Fortress.

———. 1971. *New Testament theology.* London: SCM.

Jewett, Paul K. 1988. Systematic theology 1: TH 511. Course notes presented at Fuller Theological Seminary, Pasadena, CA.

Jordan, Ivan. 1984.

Joseph, Franklin. 1987. Report for World Vision, India. Unpublished manuscript in personal files of Harry Box.

Kelber, Werner H. 1983. *The oral and the written gospel.* Philadelphia: Fortress.

Kennedy, Rod. 1983. Drama, a dynamic teacher. *Notes from the Didjeridu* (November). Berrimah, Australia: Summer Institute of Linguistics.

Keysser, Christian. 1980. *A people reborn.* Trans. Alfred Allen and John Kuder. Pasadena: William Cary Library.

Kittel, Gerhard, ed. 1964. *Theological dictionary of the New Testament*, vol. 2. Grand Rapids: Eerdmans.

Klem, Herbert V. 1982. *Oral communication of the Scripture.* Pasadena: William Carey Library.

Kluckholm, Clyde. 1949. *Mirror for man: The relationship of anthropology to modern life.* New York: McGraw-Hill.

Knowles, M. S. 1984. *The adult learner: A neglected species*, 3rd ed. Houston: Gulf.

Koehler, Paul F. 2010. *Telling God's stories with power.* Pasadena: William Carey Library.

Kraft, Charles H. 1978. Interpreting in cultural context. *Journal of Evangelical Theological Society* 21, no. 4: 357–67.

———. 1979a. *Christianity in culture.* New York: Orbis Books.

———. 1979b. *Communicating the gospel God's way.* Pasadena: William Carey Library.

———. 1983. *Communication theory for Christian witness.* Nashville: Abingdon.

Kraft, Marguerite G. 1978. *Worldview and the communication of the gospel.* Pasadena: William Carey Library.

Langness, L. L. 1974. *The study of culture.* San Francisco: Chandler & Sharp.

LaSor, William S., David A. Hubbard, and Frederick W. Bush. 1982. *Old Testament survey.* Grand Rapids: Eerdmans.

Lassey, William R., and Richard R. Fernandez, eds. 1976. *Leadership and social change.* La Jolla, CA: University Associates.

Laubach, Frank C. 1960. *Toward world literacy: Each one teach one.* Syracuse: University Press.

Leggatt, T. Watt. 1896. *Agnes C. P. Watt: 25 years mission life on Tanna.* Edinburgh: John Menzies.

Levy-Bruhl, Lucien. 1966. *How natives think.* New York: Washington Square Press.

Lindfors, Bernth, and O. Owomoyela. 1973. *Yoruba proverbs.* Athens, OH: Ohio University Center for International Studies.

Lingenfelter, Sherwood G., and Marvin K. Mayers. 1987. *Ministering cross-culturally.* Grand Rapids: Baker Book House.

Linton, Calvin. 1979. The Bible as literature. In *Expositors Bible Commentary*, vol. 1, ed. Frank E. Gaebelein. Grand Rapids: Zondervan.

Livingston, G. Herbert. 1987. *The Pentateuch in its cultural environment*, 2nd ed. Grand Rapids: Baker Book House.

Lord, Albert B. 1960. *The singer of tales.* Harvard Studies in Comparative Literature 24. Cambridge, MA: Harvard University Press.

MacKellar, Dorothea. 1981. My country. In *Enjoying poetry*, ed. Rex K. Sadler, Thomas A. S. Hayllar, and Clifford J. Powell. Melbourne: Macmillan.

Malone, Susan. 1985. Literacy program that fits: Non-formal education in a non-"Literate Society." Unpublished manuscript, Fuller Theological Seminary, Pasadena, CA.

———. 1987a. Factors which affect the development of *tokples* education programmes. In *Developing* tokples *education programmes in Papua New Guinea.* Ukarumpa, Papua New Guinea: Summer Institute of Linguistics.

———. 1987b. Guide for developing a long-range plan for TPE programmes. In *Developing* tokples *education programmes in Papua New Guinea.* Ukarumpa, Papua New Guinea: Summer Institute of Linguistics.

———. 1989. Literacy programme planning workshop: Strategies for developing multi-language literacy programmes. *Read* 24, no. 2: 2–15.

Markandaya, Kamala. 1982. *Nectar in a sieve.* New York: New American Library.

Marshall, I. Howard. 1977. *I believe in the historical Jesus.* Grand Rapids: Eerdmans.

Martin, Ralph P. 1975. *New Testament foundations*, vol. 1. Grand Rapids: Eerdmans.

McElhanon K. A., ed. 1974. *Legends from Papua New Guinea.* Ukarumpa, Papua New Guinea: Summer Institute of Linguistics.

———. 1982. *From the mouths of the ancestors.* Ukarumpa, Papua New Guinea: Summer Institute of Linguistics.

McGavran, Donald A. 1980. *Understanding church growth*, rev. ed. Grand Rapids: Eerdmans.

McGregor, Donald E. 1982. *The fish and the Cross.* Goroka, Papua New Guinea: Melanesian Institute.

McLuhan, Marshall. 1966. *Understanding media: The extensions of man.* New York: McGraw-Hill.

———. 1969. *The Gutenberg galaxy.* New York: Signet.

Miller, Charles. 1985. *Missions and missionaries in the Pacific.* New York: Edwin Millen.

Moore, George Foot. 1946. *Judaism*, vols. 1–2. Cambridge, MA: Harvard University Press.

Muench, Paul. 1984. The dynamics of history related to the work of mission. PhD diss., Fuller Theological Seminary.

Mui-Lan Tay, ed. 1985. Bible cassettes important in Africa. *ASIACOM* 3, no. 6 (June). Singapore.

Nasution, Amir. 1972. *From traditional to functional literacy and development*. Ibadan: Ibadan University Press.

Nicholls, Kathleen. 1983. *Asian arts and Christian hope*. New Delhi: Select Books.

Nida, Eugene A. 1954. *Customs and cultures*. New York: Harper & Row. Reprinted 1975 by William Carey Library.

———. 1960. *Message and mission*. New York: Harper & Row. Reprinted 1972 by William Carey Library.

Niehoff, Richard O., and Kenneth L. Neff. 1977. *Non-formal education and the rural poor*. East Lansing: Michigan State University.

Oatridge, Desmond. 1975.

Ollerenshaw, Lloyd. 1986. Outback Easter. *Vision* (August/September). Sydney: Australian Baptist Missionary Society.

Olson, Bruce. 1978. *Bruchko* (formerly titled *For this cross I'll kill you*). Carol Stream, IL: Creation House.

Ong, Walter J. 1969. World as view and world as event. *American Anthropologist* 71 (August): 634–47.

———. 1981. *The presence of the Word*. Minneapolis: University of Minnesota Press. First published 1967 by Yale University Press.

———. 1982. *Orality and literacy*. New York: Methuen.

Parry, Adam, ed. 1971. *The making of Homeric verse: The collected papers of Millman Parry*. Oxford: Clarendon.

Paterson, A. B. 1987. *The Man from Snowy River and other verses*, rev. ed. North Ryde. Australia: Angus & Robertson. First published 1961.

Peabody, Berkley. 1975. *The winged word: A study in the technique of ancient Greek oral composition as seen principally through Hesiod's* Works and Days. Albany, NY: State University of New York Press.

Pearson, Emil. 1977. *People of the aurora*. San Diego: Beta Books.

Philips, Susan Urmston. 1983. *The invisible culture*. New York: Longman.

Primrose, Robert. 1976. *Discipling non-literates: A study report*. Kenya: Daystar Communications.

Pye, Lucian W. 1967. Communication operation in non-Western societies. In *Reader in public opinion and communication*, 2nd ed., ed. Bernard Berelson and Morris Janowitz. New York: Free Press.

Rad, Gerhard von. 1960. *Old Testament theology*, vols. 1–2. New York: Harper & Row.

Redfield, Robert. 1953. *The primitive world and its transformations*. Ithaca, NY: Cornell University Press.

Richardson, Don. 1974. *The peace child*. Glendale, CA: Regal Books.

————. 1977. *Lords of the earth*. Glendale, CA: Regal Books.

————. 1981. *Eternity in their hearts*. Ventura: Regal Books.

Riesenfeld, Harald. 1957. *The gospel tradition and its beginnings*. London: A. R. Mowbray.

Riesman, David. 1960. The oral and written traditions. In *Explorations in communication*, ed. Edmund Carpenter and Marshall McLuhan. Boston: Beacon.

Rogers, Everett M., and F. Floyd Shoemaker. 1983. *The diffusion of innovations*, rev. ed. New York: Free Press.

Samovar, G. A., and R. E. Porter. 1985. *Intercultural communication: A reader*, 4th ed. Belmont, CA: Wadsworth.

Sapir, Edward. 1964. *Culture, language and personality*. Berkeley and Los Angeles: University of California Press.

Scheub, Harold. 1977. Body and image in oral narrative performance. *New Literary History* 8: 345–67.

Schwartz, Tony. 1972. *The responsive chord*. New York: Anchor.

Shaw, R. Daniel. 1988. *Transculturation*. Pasadena: William Carey Library.

Shuter, Robert. 1985. The Hmong of Laos: Orality, communication and acculturation. In *Intercultural communication: A reader*, ed. Larry Samovar and Richard Porter. Belmont, CA: Wadsworth.

Smalley, William A. 1978. *Readings in missionary anthropology*, vol. 2. Pasadena: William Carey Library.

Smith, Alex G. 2008. Communication and continuity through oral transmission. In *Communicating Christ through story and song: Orality in Buddhist contexts*, ed. Paul De Neui, 2–26. Pasadena: William Carey Library.

Søgaard, Viggo B. 1975. *Everything you need to know for a cassette ministry*. Minneapolis: Bethany Fellowship.

————. 1987. Audio cassettes help projects meet goals. *Together* (July–September). Melbourne: World Vision.

————. 1988. Communication strategy: MB546. Course notes presented at Fuller Theological Seminary, Pasadena, CA.

Soggin, J. Alberto. 1976. *Introduction to the Old Testament*. Philadelphia: Fortress.

Spruth, Erwin. 1981. And the word of God spread: A brief history of the Gutnius Lutheran Church, PNG. DMiss diss., Fuller Theological Seminary.

Streeter, B. H. 1933. Poems of Jesus. *The Hibbert Journal* 32 (October): 9–16.

Teselle, Sallie. 1975. *Speaking in parables: A study in metaphor and theology*. Philadelphia: Fortress.

Third Lausanne Congress on World Evangelisation. 2011. *The Cape Town commitment*, ed. Julia Cameron. Peabody, MA: Hendrickson, 2011.

Tippett, Alan R. 1962. Church planting in New Guinea and Papua. Unpublished manuscript, Institute of Church Growth, Eugene, OR.

————. 1967. *Solomon Islands Christianity*. Pasadena: William Carey Library.

————. 1970. *Church growth and the word of God*. Grand Rapids: Eerdmans.

————. 1973a. *Aspects of Pacific ethnohistory*. Pasadena: William Carey Library.

————. 1973b. *Verdict theology in missionary theory*. Pasadena: William Carey Library.

———. 1977. *Deep sea canoe*. Pasadena: William Carey Library

———. 1980. *Oral tradition and ethnohistory*. Canberra, Australia: St. Mark's Library.

Toffler, Alvin. 1970. *Future shock*. New York: Bantam Books.

———. 1980. *The third wave*. New York: William Morrow.

Toyotome, Masume. 1953. Poetic images and forms in the sayings of Jesus. PhD diss., Columbia University.

———. 1963. The poetry of Jesus. Unpublished manuscript, William Carey International University, Pasadena, CA.

Van Rensberg, Patrick. 1979. *Visual aids for nonformal education*. Amherst: University of Massachusetts.

Vicedom, George. 1961. *Church and people in New Guinea*. New York: Associated Press.

Wagner, C. Peter. 1987. *Strategies for church growth*. Ventura, CA: Regal Books.

Ward, Ted W., and William A. Herzog Jr. 1974. *Effective learning in non-formal education*. East Lansing: Michigan State University.

Weber, H. R. 1957. *The communication of the gospel to illiterates*. London: SCM.

Wench, Ida. 1961. *Mission to Melanesia*. London: Elek Books.

Wendell, Margaret M. 1982. *Bootstrap literature: Preliterate societies do it themselves*. Dallas: Summer Institute of Linguistics.

Whitbourne, John. 1984.

Whiteman, Darrel. 1983. *Melanesians and missionaries*. Pasadena: William Carey Library.

Whorf, Benjamin L. 1940. Science and linguistics. *Technological Review* 42: 229–41, 247–48.

Wiseman, William H. 1987a. The development of a dynamic model of communication reception. MA thesis, Wheaton College.

———. 1987b. *Oral information processing*. Unpublished manuscript, Wheaton Graduate School, Wheaton, Illinois.

INDEX